This isn't just another marriage book. *The Rhythm of Us* is an invitation—or maybe the word is
marriage you long for. Chris and J
incredibly powerful tools in the ha
saving questions, practices, and rh
dreaming of the marriage you desire and what it looks like to
pursue that dream in the here and now.

> CHRISTY NOCKELS, worship leader, songwriter, author of *The Life You Long For*

Chris and Jenni's winsome book is chock-full of wisdom, complete with practical steps to help you find your way into the unique rhythms that will make your marriage flourish.

> JOHN and STASI ELDREDGE, *New York Times* bestselling authors

I have always believed that marriage books are the hardest to write because anyone who is or has been married knows exactly how much work a good marriage requires. People want real answers and practical solutions to building a healthier, happier marriage and aren't interested in a bunch of well-meaning platitudes or clichés. In *The Rhythm of Us*, Jenni and Chris Graebe have written what I truly believe is one of the greatest marriage books I have read. It's honest and real, full of practical tips and exercises that will help strengthen your marriage and help you and your spouse grow closer as you learn how to find your rhythm as a couple. You will be challenged and encouraged as you turn each page of this book and end it feeling like you've just made a wise new couple friend you can't wait to have over for dinner.

> MELANIE SHANKLE, *New York Times* bestselling author

Marriage has been the source of both our deepest struggles and our deepest healing. Chris and Jenni offer their own hard-won wisdom, reminding us our good/hard relationships are so worth fighting for.

KATHERINE and JAY WOLF, authors of *Hope Heals* and *Suffer Strong*

I absolutely love *The Rhythm of Us*. It's inspiring. It's empowering. It's equipping. Jenni and Chris cast a clear vision for a thriving marriage that is biblical, beautiful, bountiful, and—because of grace—achievable. Written with an "us too," not a "how to" tone, you'll find yourself delightfully eager to create your own transforming "rhythm of us" with your spouse!

JEANNIE CUNNION, author of *Don't Miss Out*

I have always admired Chris and Jenni and their obvious connection. After reading this book, I understand why they are one special couple: Their marriage is clearly based in healthy rhythms! It's a must-read for any couple that is seeking a great marriage. I love this practical and profound guide for a great marriage. I'm so thankful Chris and Jenni have shared their secret sauce with all of us! This is an excellent resource for any couple just beginning or those married for many years. This admirable couple understands the ups and downs of marriage and offers a profound yet practical way to grow together through healthy rhythms.

COURTNEY DEFEO, author of *In This House, We Will Giggle* and *Treasured* study

No matter your season, married or single, this book is for you! It's a brilliant guide on creating rhythms for a healthy, life-giving marriage. God's desire for us is strong relationships, and this book gives amazing tools on how to cultivate, nurture, and protect that.

MESHALI MITCHELL, photographer, host of *A Thousand Words*, founder of A House God Is Building

Jenni and Chris welcome us into real-life relationship, opening the conversation to everyone from a *his* and *her*— as well as an *us*—perspective. This isn't a right-way or a do-this-and-get-that handbook but an invitation to learn about, practice, and lean into relationship rhythms that are as powerful as they are gentle. *The Rhythm of Us* addresses marriage, but its insight and tips prove beneficial to all our relationships.

KAY WYMA, blogger, vodcaster, author of *The Peace Project*

The Rhythm of Us comes through a distinct door that separates it from most writings on marriage. It's not only biblical and honest but is actually doable. *The Rhythm of Us* gives us practical handles to see our marriages transformed. These pages create what the Graebes call "Team Us," igniting the next exciting chapter of any marriage.

MARK and JAN FOREMAN, authors of *Never Say No* and parents of Jon and Tim Foreman of Switchfoot

It only takes a few minutes to realize that Jenni and Chris have a special relationship, and their advice and intentionality are a gift to other marriages. We're all trying to figure out a rhythm that allows us to thrive as individuals, spouses, and families—and this book will be invaluable as we navigate the days and years to come. I'm so grateful for a resource that I can confidently pass along to others, knowing that it will quickly become a favorite!

> ANGIE SMITH, bestselling author of *Seamless*

No matter where you are or what you've gone through, *The Rhythm of Us* is for you. It can help you make a good thing great or help raise a struggling relationship to a healthier rhythm. A must-read for any couple!

> ALLI WORTHINGTON, business coach, speaker, author of *Standing Strong*

Chris and Jenni have written a must-read for any married couple. . . . *The Rhythm of Us* gives a practical road map for a thriving marriage. We loved it!

> ANDREW EAST, NFL player, and SHAWN JOHNSON EAST, Olympic gymnast

If marriages ever needed renewal, it's now, and the path to renewal begins with rhythms. In *The Rhythm of Us*, Chris and Jenni warmly welcome us into their home, their struggles, and their committed journey to create a healthy marriage amid the demands of life, children, and never-ceasing distractions. We love this book and believe it will encourage you to stay the course, get creative, and find a vision of "us" that brings out the best in your marriage.

> GABE and REBEKAH LYONS, authors and hosts of *Rhythms for Life* podcast

THE RHYTHM OF US

CHRIS & JENNI GRAEBE

THE RHYTHM OF US

CREATE THE THRIVING MARRIAGE YOU LONG FOR

NavPress

A NavPress resource published in alliance
with Tyndale House Publishers

NavPress ◖

NavPress is the publishing ministry of The Navigators, an international Christian organization and leader in personal spiritual development. NavPress is committed to helping people grow spiritually and enjoy lives of meaning and hope through personal and group resources that are biblically rooted, culturally relevant, and highly practical.

For more information, visit NavPress.com.

To our children:

Kaden, Addie, Averi, Kennedi, and Keris

You are the light of our life!

May you be ever growing in the rhythms

that draw you closer and closer

toward God and toward each other.

CONTENTS

WE WON'T GET THERE BY ACCIDENT

God ordained a rhythm for this life. A dance
between the holy and the human.

EUGENE PETERSON

Tell me, what is it you plan to do
with your one wild and precious life?

MARY OLIVER

Teach us to number our days,
that we may gain a heart of wisdom.

PSALM 90:12

JENNI

For almost forty years now, I've been studying couples. Well,
thirty-nine, to be exact. I have no idea why or when it started,
but for as long as I can remember, I've been an obsessive observer
of relationships. I was totally that kid. At home, at school, at
church, out in the world around me, always taking great notice
of the marriages I encountered, especially those that seemed

to truly thrive. You know the ones I'm talking about—those couples who are somehow still wildly in love after decades of marriage. It's undeniable. You can see it every time his eyes light up when she walks into the room, in the way she laughs at his cheesy jokes, or simply in how they seem to genuinely enjoy each other.

I remember making constant mental notes about these happy couples I observed along the way. Something deep down inside me knew if I wanted a marriage like that, I needed to start paying great attention. Every time I encountered a couple that spoke to the deep longing within me, I found myself making a new mental note. I even started a list in the back of my Bible of things to look for in my future husband. (Cheesy, I know. Anyone else do this?)

What I didn't realize God was doing throughout all those years, with every mental note taken, was giving me an invaluable gift. He was teaching me the rhythms of a thriving marriage, the kind of marriage we all dream of having. As it turns out, this kind of marriage isn't only meant for a select few. While every relationship is different, bringing its own unique set of struggles, needs, and desires to the table, what I have discovered after a lifetime of studying couples, from friends and family and mentors and leaders to world-renowned authors and speakers Chris and I have the privilege of interviewing on our podcast is that, underneath it all, the best relationships share the same basic rhythms.

Underneath it all, the best relationships share the same basic rhythms.

Throughout our time together, we'll unpack what those core essential rhythms are, how they work, and the results they can have on our relationships if we choose to practice them. We'll also spend some time uncovering your unique rhythms as a couple and how, as you become aware of them, you can begin to transform your marriage by intentionally filling your life with the things you both value most.

CHRIS ————————————————————————————————

Jenni and I are just two weeks apart in age. (I'm older and like to remind her.) We're both Xennials—part of that tiny generation tucked right in between Millennials and Gen Xers.[1] We have fond memories of the fifteen-foot cord hanging from the family telephone on the kitchen wall, we printed directions off MapQuest, and we took great pride in our CD collections. Though we didn't meet until we were twenty-one, we experienced the world around us in a very similar way, due to being almost the exact same age. In many ways, it's felt as though God was intentionally weaving our lives together from the very beginning.

Long before we ever met, our lives were full of uncanny similarities. We are both headstrong firstborns, with only a younger brother for a sibling; our parents separated when we were around six years old; we both had roommates that moved out halfway through our freshman year of college, leaving us with the highly coveted single-occupant room; and we both spent spring break of that freshman year having too much fun in Panama City. But maybe the craziest similarity is that during high school, we each stumbled into an empty classroom (me in Indiana, Jenni in Texas) to find the same rude comment written underneath our full names on an empty chalkboard. (I know. Weird, right?)

The most important similarity we share, however, is that God massively changed both of our lives just before we met at the age of twenty-one. One was a "Yankee" (me) and the other was a smokin'-hot Southern blonde from the great state of Texas (not me). But one fact was strikingly the same: We were both desperately broken and in need of a Savior. Through His grace, God lovingly pulled us out of our mess, rescued us from the dangerous trajectory we were on, and set us on a brand-new path that would thankfully include meeting each other.

Despite all the overlap in our lives, there was one key area that remained drastically different: the view we developed of marriage in our early years. After a brief separation, Jenni's parents chose to reunite and have actually been married for over forty years now. Mine, however, did not. Over my life, I have had four dads and three moms, including a smattering of stepparents who came in and out of my life throughout the years. I experienced firsthand the detrimental effects divorce can have on a child.

I don't fault my parents—I know life isn't easy. And through God's grace, I'm grateful to say, both of my parents have since found amazing spouses and are now happily married. But needless to say, I didn't reach adulthood with the healthiest understanding of what a thriving marriage could look like.

I knew there had to be a better way, and I was determined to find it.

But here's how God has redeemed this part of my story and used it to shape who I am today. Just like Jenni, I was paying careful attention to the notable marriages around me—except while Jenni was noticing what *to* do, I was learning what *not* to do. The heartbreaking examples I observed along the way ignited a passionate resolve in me to make my own mental list of things I refused to do in my future marriage.

When I look across the landscape of my early years, it's hard for me to think of a married couple that I wanted to emulate. I didn't understand the concept of being in "rhythm" with your spouse, but I had a pretty clear understanding of what it meant to be "out of rhythm." I knew there had to be a better way, and I was determined to find it.

What Jenni and I have both learned about creating a thriving marriage is that we won't get there by accident. As a kid, it's pretty easy to keep a running list of all the specific things you do and don't want in your future marriage. But intentionally living them out as an adult in your own actual marriage? That's a horse of a different color. Thriving together in a life we love doesn't just happen. It takes developing intentional rhythms that guide us into the life and marriage we long for. As pastor and theologian Eugene Peterson said, "What kingfishers and falling stones and chiming bells do without effort requires development on our part, a formation into who we truly are."[2]

> We won't get there by accident.

THE RULE OF LIFE
JENNI

When we enter into marriage, we each carry with us our own unique vision for our life together that we bring to the relationship. Throughout our time together, we will begin to bring those visions to the surface and see how they line up. No marriage can thrive when our eyes are consistently focused on ourselves. Together we'll learn to shift our focus from just our own lives to noticing, nurturing, and supporting the work God is up to in our spouse, as well. There are a thousand different ways we could choose to live our life together. But to create a thriving marriage, we must intentionally center our lives around rhythms that lead us toward God and toward each other. In other words, we need to develop a "rule of life" for our marriage.

No marriage can thrive when our eyes are consistently focused on ourselves.

What is a rule of life? I'm so glad you asked! It's not as crazy as it sounds; I promise. Stick with me. Maybe you've already heard this term floating around spiritual circles, or maybe you haven't heard it at all. But either way, don't let the word *rule* intimidate you—crafting a rule of life is a simple, practical tool that absolutely anyone can use.

In spiritual formation, the ancient practice of developing a rule of life—or what I like to call a "rhythm of life"—essentially involves envisioning the person we want to become and the specific life we feel called to live, then crafting a set of personal habits to guide us toward that place. Not a list of rigid rules, but something more like a trellis supporting the growth of a budding vine, our rhythm supports intentional movement and growth toward the life we long to live. A rule of life is an intentional plan for what we will do with our "one wild and precious life."[3] As Andy Crouch so simply puts it, our rhythm of life is "a set of practices to guard our hearts and guide our lives."[4]

When I first learned about this idea of crafting a rule of life, I fell in love with this beautiful, life-changing practice. Taking the time to evaluate my life allowed me to realize which habits needed to go and which needed to stay, which relationships needed pruning and which needed nurturing.

Light bulbs came on, allowing me to prioritize the parts of life that were crucial to my overall well-being. Habits such as running through the trees, savoring the sacred morning hour, and enjoying time at the table each night with my people—I realized these are not just occasional hobbies I wish I could enjoy more of; they are actually crucial to my spiritual growth, worthy of prioritizing.

But as I began cultivating and following my new rhythm of life, I began to notice that something wasn't quite right: It was still all about me. The truth is, because I am married, I have the responsibility to consider my spouse and his journey as well. As John Eldredge puts it, "You are the most powerful person in your spouse's life. You are *the* greatest instrument of redemption in their world."[5] It's not enough to focus on my own thriving alone. I have been given the remarkable gift of a spouse, entrusted with the honor and privilege to care for, notice, and support him as he attempts every day to grow and thrive in his own walk with Christ. In marriage, we're no longer two but *one* (see Matthew 19:6). So, in crafting our rhythm of life, we must include and consider our other half as well. Practicing a "rhythm of me" doesn't cut it. We need a "rhythm of us" in order to move toward the life we long for.

> Practicing a "rhythm of me" doesn't cut it. We need a "rhythm of us" in order to move toward the life we long for.

We will never be content living only for ourselves. To move toward my best self requires that I not only examine my own life-giving rhythms but that I consider Chris's, as well. What makes him come alive? What keeps him healthy and feeling at home in our life together? What rhythms draw us closer to one another?

These are things I want to know, things I *need* to know. Because he is a part of me, my rhythm is no longer complete without his. Part of my rhythm needs to be prioritizing his flourishing, as well as my own.

At a wedding, Dietrich Bonhoeffer once gave this beautiful advice to a young couple: "Today you are young and very much in love and you think that your love can sustain your marriage. It can't. Let your marriage sustain your love."[6] As we will learn more in depth throughout our time together, this kind of rich, mature, thriving love that we all long for requires not only deep desire but also intentional direction. The consistent rhythms we choose to fill our marriage and life with will either stoke the fire of that initial flame or eventually snuff it out completely.

I am convinced that becoming the kind of couple that stays wildly in love means we must develop a rhythm of life that will lead us continually toward God and toward each other. As writer and teacher Ronald Rolheiser puts it, "What sustains a relationship long-term is ritual, routine, a regular rhythm that incarnates the commitment."[7] But how do we do that? Where do we even begin? We start by examining where we are. As Margaret Guenther says, "Before we can formulate a wise rule for our lives, we need to take a hard look at ourselves and ask, 'What is the shape of my life right now? What does my stewardship of time, energy, substance, and creativity look like?'"[8]

Whether we realize it or not, we already have a "rhythm of us." The question is, where is it taking us? Do we like the couple our rhythm is shaping us to become? And if not, how do we change it?

Over our time together, we'll take a look at that current

life rhythm—because knowing where we are helps us discover where we want to go. Our goal throughout this journey is not to provide you with a weekly schedule you should follow but rather to offer a simple guide to examine the rhythms that are contributing to the couple you're becoming. Together, we'll learn some essential healthy habits true of every thriving marriage. We'll let go of the habits that keep leading us into ruts. And lastly, we'll uncover the unique rhythms you and your spouse have as a couple that draw you closer to God and closer to each other.

> Whether we realize it or not, we already have a "rhythm of us."

I don't know about you, but I don't want to live a life of just skimming by. I don't want to merely survive each week, or just drift wherever the current of the world decides to take me. I want to become one of those "wildly in love for decades" kind of couples I admired as a kid. I want us to strengthen each other's life and faith over our years together. I want to cultivate the kind of marriage, family, and life that my kids' wildest dreams are made of. I want to be one of those couples for *them* that would stop the younger me in my tracks. Through God's grace, I want the love we share to become a light to those around us in our community.

The rhythms we create will also live on well beyond our years. When our kids grow up and leave home to enter the world and find spouses of their own, what rhythms will they take with them? What dream of life together will they carry in their hearts? Will they be able to say, "I want a love like that!"? It's the most important gift we can give them. We could get almost everything else wrong in life and in parenting, but if our kids know deep down to their core that Mom and Dad are passionately in love with God and crazy about each other, we're supplying them with the most significant legacy possible.

God has entrusted us with the incredible gift of life *together*. What will we choose to do with it? Developing a rhythm for our marriage is a plan to steward well the precious gift of each other. As Margaret Guenther writes, "If we are to be good stewards of our abundance of time, energy, and creativity, we need to live in awareness. We need a rule, not to hem us in but to enable us to flourish."[9] Crafting our rhythm will give us the tools we need to live with intention, remind us of the life we want to build together, and gently guide us to grow closer to Christ and to each other.

So, we invite you to take this journey with us toward a thriving marriage, toward becoming one of those "still wildly in love after decades" kind of couples. As we begin this journey together, with God as our unwavering guide, we'll learn together what a thriving marriage looks like and the practices that will get us there. **There are a thousand different ways we could choose to live our life together. The goal is to intentionally center our lives around the rhythms that lead us toward God and toward each other.**

May these essential rhythms we unpack together be as lifegiving to you as they have been to us. May the Lord use these powerful practices to lift you and carry you from wherever these words currently find you—to the marriage you've only dreamed of.

Here's to the beginning of a beautiful journey.

Here's to the miracle of marriage.

Here's to *the rhythm of us*.

PRACTICE

- Name some couples you admire for their thriving relationship.

- What healthy rhythms have you noticed in the couples you admire?

- What unhealthy rhythms have you learned to avoid or reject?

- As we begin this journey together, offer a prayer of gratitude for the gift of having a spouse to love and ask the Lord for guidance and wisdom to steward this great gift well.

PART ONE

NAMING
WHERE WE ARE

THE FIRST IMPORTANT STEP in any worthwhile journey is *naming where we are*. Before we can determine where we want to go and the healthy rhythms we want to fill our life with, it's important to take a good, long look at where we actually are. Who do we want to become together? What kind of life do we long to build? What choices are we consistently making? Where have we drifted from our highest values? Where do we wish things could be different?

Before we can fill our lives with the rhythms we value most, it's important to identify the practices we don't. Moving toward a thriving marriage means getting on the same page about where we want to go, unlearning unhealthy rhythms, and discovering what might be missing. In this section, we'll learn more about how we fall out of rhythm in the first place, the dangerous ruts to avoid, and how to craft a vision for the couple we want to become in the future.

1

THE FUTURE US

Starting with a Vision

We were together, I forget the rest.

PARAPHRASE OF WALT WHITMAN

JENNI

A few weeks ago, a friend of mine hosted a beautiful gathering for her daughter's high school graduation. She had a wonderful celebration planned for her senior, including a lovely round table filled with all the things that represented eighteen years of life for her precious young daughter on the brink of adulthood. Pictures of family and close friends; tiny, stamped footprints and baby rattles; playbills and vinyl records; a pair of old cowboy boots; faded summer-camp T-shirts. The cherished treasures that make up a young life. Tears immediately sprang to my eyes as I glanced over each item on her table, and a question arose from somewhere deep within me: *What do you want on your table?*

So many tables to fill. An anniversary table after decades of loving each other well. What does that table look like? A graduation table for each of our five kiddos, eighteen years in the making. Gah. What does that table look like? My own table, at the end of a life well lived. What do I want that table to look like?

Before we can craft a rhythm of us, we first must envision the *future* us. What do we want on our table? What does the future *us* look like? Who do we hope to become twenty, thirty, forty years from now? When they leave our home, what will our kids say about the love they watched us share? What kind of relationship do we long to enjoy together? The truth is, the habits we choose to practice today will determine the couple we become tomorrow.

Our rhythms determine our future. The strength, of course, is not in the rhythms themselves, but in the people they can lead us to become. Before we can craft a rhythm of us, we first must envision our future together. Getting specific about your vision of the future takes it out of fantasy land and into a reachable goal. Looking at a clear picture of the future allows us to evaluate the things we're doing now and determine which habits will take us there and which will not.

> The habits we choose to practice today will determine the couple we become tomorrow.

We each get a set of tables. I have my own, one for my marriage, and one for my family. That's it. Those are all the tables I get, the only ones I am invited to fill. You have your own tables to fill. Stop for a moment. If you can, sit quietly, and close your eyes for a few seconds. Think about the tables in your life, and envision each of them in the future.

At the end of your life, what do you hope your tables will look like? When your friends and family gather to celebrate your fifty-year wedding anniversary, what do you hope to find on that table? Who do you want to see around it? Take a moment and write down your vision. Get as specific as you can.

What's on Your Future Table?

YOUR ACTUAL TABLE

CHRIS ——————————————————————————————————

Now that we've got a clear vision for the future, let's take a moment to examine where we currently find ourselves. What is the shape of my table in this current season of my life? What does it look like? Are there things I want to remove? Things that need redemption? Things I wish to add? What am I waiting for?

All change begins with honesty. If we want to grow, we need to first take a good, hard look at where we are now. Not where we are in our heads, where we wish we could be, or where we were one Friday night three years ago. Something shifts when we admit and locate exactly where we find ourselves in this current moment. Maybe it's been a while since you've had this conversation with your spouse, or maybe it's never happened at all. It's time to get brutally honest.

Take a moment and rate on the line below where you'd say you and your spouse are on a scale from miserable to thriving. If your biggest conflict is over who left the peanut butter out or whose turn it is to do the dishes, you're probably closer to the thriving side. But if you can't go a day without fighting, can't remember the last time you had sex, and find it difficult just to be in the same room together, I'm guessing you're closer to miserable. (Of course, conflict is a part of every relationship, including thriving ones. But conflict that is constant or that degrades and dehumanizes is never a sign of a healthy marriage.)

←—————————————————————————————————————→

MISERABLE   THRIVING

We can only grow to the degree we are honest. The healing process can only begin in areas where we've taken the time to truthfully admit our lack and our pain. It's important that we assess the quality of our relationship based on what is *actually true* rather than what we *wish* were true. How we *actually feel* as opposed to how we *think* we should feel. As Larry Crabb says, "God meets us where we are, not where we pretend to be."[1]

Take some time to discuss with your spouse where you are as a couple, free of judgment. This is not an invitation to point out each other's flaws. As much as you can, with grace and openness and a desire to move your marriage closer to the thriving end of the scale, honestly assess your marriage.

- Where do each of you feel in and out of rhythm?
- What words would you use to describe your relationship in its current state?
- How would other key people in your life describe your relationship?
- What does your current table look like?

One thing I have found extremely helpful in this practice of naming is to pay attention to the areas I find myself continually thinking, *This shouldn't matter so much to me*, or, *I really shouldn't feel this way*. If I am continually tempted to "shouldn't" away my feelings, that usually means it's pointing to something important. As the song goes, "If it matters, let it matter."[2] Sometimes we need to give ourselves permission to allow what's bothering us to finally surface, so that we can begin to change it.

Throughout our time together, we will keep a continual finger on the pulse of where we are, identify where we want to be, and practice the rhythms that will take us there. Wherever you find yourself right now on the relational scale, whether deeply in rhythm or significantly out of rhythm, be encouraged. Truth frees. Honestly admitting where we are is the greatest catalyst for change to begin. As the apostle John once wrote, "You will know the truth, and the truth will set you free" (John 8:32).

Take a moment to write it out. Be as specific as you can. This is only for you and your spouse. Resist the urge to judge wherever you may be today. Remember, naming and acknowledging where we are is the first, important step in the right direction.

What's on Your Current Table?

THE POWER OF PRAYER

JENNI ─────────────────────────────────

Something strange happens every once in a while, during the night when our daughter is fast asleep. If you also happen to be the parent of a tween daughter, you may be familiar with this delightful little dance yourself. Before putting her to bed, we help her pick out her clothes and hang them neatly on the dresser, ready for morning. Then somehow, mysteriously during the night, something switches in her brain. When she awakens, she has no recollection of choosing said outfit and decides she *must* instead wear a stained pajama shirt paired with track shorts in the middle of winter. All manner of sobs ensue as she is told she cannot wear summer clothes in December and that she must instead stick with the outfit she chose when she was in her right mind the night before. Tears. Stomps. Pouts. Out the door.

> Honestly admitting where we are is the greatest catalyst for change to begin.

This is my least favorite way to start a morning. And here's the thing—having four girls, I'm very familiar with this rhythm (or, actually, this rut). I know by the time we pull up to the school and she sees her friends, by the time she's fully awake and her breakfast has settled, she'll forget all about her outfit frustrations and jump joyfully into her morning. By the end of the day, she will even lie in bed with me and laugh at how absurd her morning antics were. Yes, by bedtime, it will all be water under the bridge. And yet, today, I let it throw off my entire morning.

I should have paused right then and there to name where I

am, recognize how I am feeling, and lay the day at the feet of the only one who can bring true healing to it. But alas, I don't. Instead, I choose to let my mind drift, becoming so preoccupied with thoughts and strategies for ending this crazy cycle that I completely lose track of time and have now pulled into the preschool drop-off with one minute to spare.

Snapping myself back to reality, I quickly gather my three-year-old's things and unbuckle her car seat. She's crying. I try to console her while moving at the speed of light (a quite impossible task, let me tell you). Too late. As I rush to the drop-off line, I am met with a sweet but sympathetic look from the preschool director. "I'm sorry. You'll have to go around the building to drop her off at the office door." I can see her class—they're all literally standing right in front of me, walking in a single-file line into the building. Nevertheless, I obediently comply.

What a morning, I think to myself as we make our way down the walk of shame to the late-parent drop-off spot. My precious three-year-old wraps her little arms around my neck, plops her beautiful blonde head on my shoulder, and I pull her close. The warm beat of her heart against mine somehow reminds me what a gift this all is—to be *her* mom, to be alive—and I finally decide to pause and offer up a silent prayer of surrender.

Oh Jesus. I've been running all morning without acknowledging you, haven't I? It's only 9:15 a.m., and I'm already in desperate need of a do-over. I don't know how I got here, but would you turn this day around, Lord? I lay it all at your feet.

As we reach the door, I put Keris down and look into her adorable blue eyes to say goodbye for the day. "I sure love you, babe." Kisses and hugs. Feeling a little better already. I sign her in as the director motions her to join her class. She turns back, launching herself around my legs for one last embrace. "I'm gonna miss you *so* much, Mommy!" Then with a smile, she happily bounces her way down the hall. Gah. Melt. Me. Completely. *Thank you, Lord. I sure needed that.*

"Hey, Jenni!" I turn around to see a sweet young couple making their way behind me on the walk of shame. We met over a year ago, right after we moved to this new city, right before COVID-19 shut the world down completely. Chris and I hadn't seen them since, but it turns out their son is in Keris's class. We enjoy a great conversation, and I am surprised at what a simple, pleasant interaction with a few lovely humans does for my spirit in the middle of this isolating pandemic.

I head to my car feeling significantly lighter than when I'd arrived, and I realize the power of a simple prayer of surrender . . . of confession, of (gulp) repentance. Something dramatically shifts the moment we pause to honestly name where we are, admit our need for God, and cry out to Him for help. A burden lifts, the atmosphere shifts, and our hearts are renewed as we finally plop our head on His shoulder and lean on Him to guide us to a better place.

> Something dramatically shifts the moment we pause to honestly name where we are, admit our need for God, and cry out to Him for help.

Unfortunately, it usually takes getting to a breaking point of significant pain to cause us to cry out for help. But we don't have to wait until we reach the bottom of the misery scale in our marriage before we cry out to the Lord for help. We can cry out right now. We can begin the healing journey now.

When's the last time you cried out? Are you at the point in your marriage where you realize you need a power greater than yourself to take you where you want to go? To bring healing where there is great pain? Have you tried everything you know to try in your own strength? True change begins with honesty. Honesty with ourselves about where we are. Honesty with our spouse about where we feel out of rhythm. And honesty with the Lord about our complete and desperate need for Him. The truth is, most marital problems are spiritual problems.[3] We must begin by crying out to the only one who has the power to save us.

Take a moment to offer a prayer of surrender for your marriage. To the One who created it. To the One who truly knows the rhythms of a thriving marriage and how to get you there better than anyone. Acknowledge your need for Him. There's a notable difference between gritting it out on our own and the healthy rhythms that naturally flow from a heart that's been strengthened by the Lord. Thank Him for the gift of someone to love for a lifetime, for the miracle of marriage, and for the good future He has for you. Acknowledge where you are today and ask Him to lead you through *His* strength to the more beautiful life He has for you.

A Prayer of Surrender

Lord Jesus, I cry out . . .

PRACTICE

- Put on a pot of good coffee and some great music. Start to dream together of what you want the future "us" to look like—twenty, thirty, forty years from now.

- Make a list of things you hope your kids will say about you as a couple when they leave your home.

- Take some time to fill in your tables on pages 17 and 21. Be as honest and specific as you possibly can. Recognizing where we are is the first step toward change.

2

IN MY HEAD

Falling Out of Rhythm

We must pay the most careful attention, therefore,
to [the truth] we have heard,
so that we do not drift away.

HEBREWS 2:1

rhythm: a strong, regular, repeated
pattern of movement or sound

CONCISE OXFORD ENGLISH DICTIONARY

CHRIS

A few years ago, Jenni and I were sitting around the circle of a new small-group gathering, each taking turns to introduce ourselves to this group of strangers. It's one of our favorite things to do—bringing a handful of people together, pouring hot cups of coffee, letting the candles burn all the way down as we take turns sharing the deep stuff of life. Something amazing takes place when we stop to listen to someone else's story.

We began the night by each rattling off the top five factors in our lives we thought would accurately describe who we were to this new group of people. Upon realizing it was his turn to share, our friend Austin quickly swallowed his snickerdoodle and said, "Let's see—well, I'm a husband of five years, a soon-to-be father, a pastor, a worship leader . . . oh, and in my head, I'm a runner . . . but really, only in my head."

Everyone laughed and nodded in agreement as Austin continued his introduction. Meanwhile, light bulbs were going off inside for me and Jenni. He had just put into words something we'd been feeling for a while. What he meant, of course, was, "running is something very important to me—something in fact, that I love very much and am actually pretty good at when I *practice* it . . . but, if you look at my current, actual life, somehow it's become something I only *used* to do. Someone I think I am, but only in my head."

We all have our own list of "in my head" identities and habits:

- "In my head, I . . . start off every morning in God's Word."
- "In my head, I . . . have sex with my spouse at least three times a week."
- "In my head, I . . . exercise every single day."
- "In my head, I . . . take my wife on a date every Saturday."

Most of the time, it happens so gradually, we don't even realize we're falling out of rhythm. We plan to get up early and enjoy some much-needed quiet time. We purchase the same salad ingredients and watch them go bad. We buy pair upon pair of running shoes. We dream about how great it would feel to be more active as a family, spend more quality time together, go on more romantic date nights, or grow closer to the Lord.

The truth is, though, unless we make room for these things to show up in our actual lives, chances are, they will remain only in our heads. And if we're not careful, years will have gone by before we realize the long list of "in my head" habits we didn't cultivate. I don't want this future for you or for me. We need a set of intentional rhythms that will help us live out the things we value most.

These days, we are more hurried and distracted than ever. We know something isn't quite right, but we're going too fast to put our finger on why. If I asked you, I'm sure you could tell me all the things you value most, and the great vision you have for your life, marriage, and family. But when you look at your current, actual life . . . does it look anything like the life you envisioned? Remember: We won't get there by accident. Thriving together in a life we love doesn't just happen.

> We need a set of intentional rhythms that will help us live out the things we value most.

As we drove home from small group that night, Jenni and I started asking each other, "What are *our* 'in my head' habits? What rhythms have we fallen out of?" A few immediately came to mind for each of us. And as we paid attention over the next few months, we began to see more and more "only in my head" patterns. Things we would have sworn were an important part of our weekly rhythms—but upon closer inspection . . . were nowhere to be found. Here's what we realized: It's very possible to drift out of the habits you value most without even realizing it.

For example, Jenni found herself both purchasing and then throwing away a lot of fresh greens every single week. Now, in her head, she drinks a green smoothie every single morning, but when she took a look at her actual life, clearly it had become

> As it turns out, thinking about doing something is not the same as actually living it out.

something she only used to do. The garbage can told us the real story. Something had changed in our lives to throw her off of this habit, without even realizing it.

As it turns out, thinking about doing something is not the same as actually living it out. We can spend so much time thinking about things we wish we could change or habits we used to practice that we can trick ourselves into thinking we are living the way we want—when the cold hard truth is, we aren't.

RESIST THE DRIFT

JENNI ——————————————————————————

This is called drifting. Living without intention. Being carried along by the current.[1] We don't want to let life just happen to us, drifting along wherever the current of the world decides to take us. We want to intentionally create a beautiful life that we love, together. We need to stop the drift.

One of my favorite Scriptures says, "Trust in the LORD and *do* good" (Psalm 37:3, emphasis mine). You and I have the unbelievable opportunity to *participate* with God in creating a life that's *good*, a life *worth living*. The Hebrew word for *do* in this verse is ʿāśâ, which also means "to offer," "to bring forth," "to prepare," "to make."[2] Keeping our hope and trust in God to do what only He can is, of course, the first step, but it can't be where we stop. It's not enough to just sit back and trust, waiting for the life and marriage we desire to come and land on our doorstep. We have also been entrusted to *act*. Commanded, in fact, to act. Trust *and* do.

While we're at it, just studying Hebrew together, let's also take a quick look at that next word in the verse: *good*, which is the Hebrew word *tôb*, meaning "beautiful," "best," "bountiful," "prosperous," and even "precious."[3] It's the same word that God uses in Genesis to describe the completion of His creation (Genesis 1:31). Think about the implications of that: Our loving God has intentionally designed us to partner with Him in the precious creation of our lives. God, in all His infinite goodness, gifted you and me with the power of choice and the ability to design a life that's beautiful. Through His great wisdom and love, He doesn't just plop us down into a thriving life; He graciously invites our active participation.

> Our loving God has intentionally designed us to partner with Him in the precious creation of our lives.

What this means for us, in regard to our marriage, is that we are never stuck. You and I get to participate in the making of our marriage. For better or worse, the rhythms we choose to consistently fill our lives with determine the couple we become and the relationship we create. Our habits stop the drift.

It's time to give yourself permission to discover the life and marriage you long for. To identify the things you value most— the rhythms that make your hearts come alive—and to ask God to show you how He's designed you to thrive together. To give yourself permission to name what you both love and to fill your life with it.

Maybe, like me, you needed that reminder today. That we are never stuck. Never powerless. Step-by-step, choice after choice, we *can* begin to change and grow toward a life and marriage that takes our breath away.

RECOVER THE DREAM

Most of us don't even realize we've been living the drifter's life until we hit a serious bump along the way to wake us up. According to author Daniel Harkavy:

> For many people, it takes a significant event—often a negative one accompanied by pain and regret—to break out of the Drift. It could be a serious diagnosis from your doctor that wakes you up to how you've been drifting in your health, or perhaps being passed over for an expected promotion at work alerts you to the fact that you've been drifting in your career. Whatever the case, events like these have a way of waking us up to what's really going on in our lives and how we may not have been living the way we intended.[4]

Eugene Peterson described his wake-up call coming in the form of the innocent words of his little girl. He had been away from his wife and family, faithfully attending to pastoral duties for thirty-eight nights in a row. He had not been counting, but his daughter, Karen, had. When she asked him to read her a bedtime story, and his response was once again, "I'm sorry, Karen, but I have a meeting tonight," she informed him it was the thirty-eighth day he had been absent from their family at bedtime.[5]

Bump. Suddenly, Eugene was wide awake to his drifting. This wake-up call pushed him to seek the Lord and his church community for a new rhythm of life, one that would allow him to stop the drift that was taking him further and further away from his wife and family and from the life he truly felt called to live as a man and as a pastor.

So how do we stop the drift and recover the dream we have for our life and for our marriage?

Naming What Matters

Anytime we go to the beach, without fail, as we splash around in the water, within just a few short minutes we can look up to see just we how far we have unintentionally drifted from where we first started out. The current is stronger than we realize. The only sure way to stay where we want to be is to somehow tether ourselves to the shore. In order to resist

> The current is stronger than we realize.

the drift, we need to be continually connected to something greater and stronger than the current. We need to keep the truth of what matters most constantly in front of us (Hebrews 2:1).

Our rhythms flow from our values. Once we name what matters most to us, we can tether ourselves to those values by intentionally putting them *first* in our lives. You've probably heard of the rocks and rice analogy. The container represents our life. The rocks represent our highest priorities, and the grains of rice represent everything else. The goal is to put the rocks into the container first, and then to pour in all the smaller grains of rice. The only way everything can fit in the container is if we put the biggest rocks (our highest values) in first. If we allow our container to first be filled with all the smallest grains of rice, there will be no room left for the largest rocks. You get the idea.

This is the solution Eugene ultimately found as he sought to protect his time and vision for his life as a pastor:

I find that when these central needs are met, there is plenty of time for everything else. . . . The only way I have found to accomplish [everything else] without resentment and anxiety is to first take care of the priorities. If there is no time to nurture these essentials, I become a busy pastor, harassed and anxious, a whining, compulsive Martha instead of a contemplative Mary.[6]

The key to stopping the drift is to protect our priorities. When we take the time to discover what we both value most, we can begin to put intentional time and energy behind them, moving us toward a life that guards and encompasses them.

The Power of Consistency

Great things are done by a series of small things brought together.
VINCENT VAN GOGH

CHRIS ——————————————————————————————

When we develop a rhythm of life, we use the power of consistency to create a path toward our desired destination. Transformation isn't just about learning new things—it's also about applying them, and more specifically, *applying them consistently*. Power is not found in doing something only once but in practicing it over and over.

- loving *consistently*
- exercising *consistently*
- being kind *consistently*
- showing thoughtfulness *consistently*

A rhythm is a strong, regular, repeated pattern of movement. Regular. Repeated. Actions only become rhythms and gain the power to change our lives when we practice them not just once but over and over. As Galatians 6:9 says, "Let us not become weary in doing good, for at the proper time we will reap a harvest if we do not give up." The harvest doesn't come when we do good just one time, here and there whenever we feel like it, or when it fits into our schedule, but in doing it again and again until the harvest comes. **The fruit is found in the not giving up.**

Water is not more powerful than rock, but over time, as the waves *consistently* crash over the solid mass, they actually begin to reshape the rock. We don't change anything by doing it once. We change by developing the habit. We don't become a spouse who loves well by bringing flowers once, or by listening to our spouse just that one Friday night. We become the spouse we long to be by consistently listening every day, by choosing to show thoughtfulness again and again. Over and over, we're developing a life of love. Step-by-step, we're becoming someone new. And as we are shaped into a person who loves well, day by day, our relationship is shaped into the marriage we long for. Small changes over time add up to build a better life. Wave upon wave upon wave smooths the stone.[7]

We don't drift our way into a thriving marriage. Our daily choices lead us to a specific destination. As author and leadership coach John C. Maxwell wrote, "You will never change your life until you change something you do daily. The secret of your success is found in your daily routine."[8] When our highest values inform our rhythms, we stop drifting and move toward the relationship we want.

There have been a lot of things I've wanted to change over the years. I've spent a lot of time wishing things would change but didn't know how to make any kind of a dent. So, because I couldn't do everything, I didn't do anything. But the truth is, we are never powerless. There is always something we can do, even if it's just one step in the right direction. The key to changing anything is doing one small thing after another, over and over, moving toward the change.

PRACTICE

- Take a minute to list some of your own "in my head" habits.

- What's something you wish you could change about your life together? What's one small action you could take today to move toward it?

- This week, ask your spouse where they feel both in and out of rhythm in your marriage.

- What important values do you sense you may be drifting from?

3

LETTING GO

From Ruts to Rhythms

Love must be sincere. Hate what is evil; cling to what is good.

ROMANS 12:9

Certain things, if not seen as lovely or detestable,
are not being correctly seen at all.

C. S. LEWIS

You can play the game, you can act out the part,
though you know it wasn't written for you.

JAMES TAYLOR

JENNI

When we got married in the summer of 2004, Chris had just finished filming a reality TV show on MTV called *Road Rules*. (If you're over the age of forty, you're probably flipping out right about now. For our under-forty friends, Google it! Except maybe not that one episode . . .) The popularity of the show launched him into a full-time speaking career, so he was traveling every week to different events, conferences, and churches, sharing his story of faith across the globe.

Those first few years following the show were quite a wild ride. I don't think either of us were fully prepared for just how much it would change our lives. Almost two decades later, I'm happy to report that he thankfully no longer gets stopped for pictures when we're in line at the grocery store or asked for autographs while we're dining at restaurants, but at the beginning of our relationship, it was pretty much a part of our weekly rhythm.

I'll never forget hearing about the first time a random girl walked by, grabbed him by the arm, and said, "Where're we going, handsome?" He and our friend John had been to a promo event, and a fan had made her way past the crowd to get to him.

"He sure loves you, Jen," John told me later that evening. "I've never seen anyone handle that kind of attention with more integrity and dignity than this man. He just quickly removed her hand, matter-of-factly said, 'I'm taken,' and then walked away."

And I have seen him handle himself this way countless times over the last seventeen years of our marriage. There was zero part of him that lingered or enjoyed or needed that kind of attention, even for a second. He has earned my trust, over and over, by the way he carries me in his heart, even when I'm not with him. I knew in that moment, and a million moments after, I could trust him completely.

> Before we can fill our lives with the rhythms we value most, it's important to identify the practices we don't.

As the philosopher Mencius once said, "Before a man can do things, there must be things he will not do." Before we can fill our lives with the rhythms we value most, it's important to identify the practices we don't. Chris did that as a child, instinctively noticing what not to do in order to have a healthy marriage. In the same way, we must name the things we absolutely refuse to do as a couple. Creating a rhythm of us is about discovering what leads us to life as well as stepping out of the ruts that keep us off track. What do we need to choose to do differently in our life now to get us where we want to be tomorrow?

REMOVE THE OBSTACLES

I love the verse in Isaiah that says, "Build up, build up, prepare the road! Remove the obstacles out of the way of my people" (Isaiah 57:14). The Hebrew word used here for *obstacle* is *mikšôl*, which also means a stumbling block, a cause for falling, or an enticement to go astray.[1] Before we can set out to fill our lives with healthy, life-giving rhythms, we first must clear out the toxins and dangers that are waiting to trip us up along the way.

You may already know exactly what's bothering you most. You need no help pinpointing the destructive cycles you've been stuck in. Most couples, when asked where they're out of rhythm, have no trouble immediately naming at least a few areas where they feel off. If that's you, go ahead and write down some of the ruts that come to mind. It's amazing how the simple act of identifying toxic patterns lets the air out of them and loosens their hold on us.

Everything exposed by the light becomes visible—and everything that is illuminated becomes a light.

EPHESIANS 5:13

When we say out loud or write down what's been bothering us most and weighing us down, we remove shame's power. I've learned this the hard way too many times.

There is no real freedom in denial, only in confession.

I can waste so much valuable time building something up in my head that it begins to feel impossibly large. By bringing it out into the light, by writing it out and surrendering it in prayer to the Lord, speaking the words out loud to my spouse or confiding in a trusted friend, the shame and darkness that overwhelms me vanishes. There is no real freedom in denial, only in confession.

> The path of life leads upward for the wise; they leave the grave behind.
>
> PROVERBS 15:24, NLT

One of the most helpful tools we've found for pinpointing the rhythms that have become ruts is a concept outlined in Dr. Henry Cloud's book *The One-Life Solution*: "Find the misery, and set the rule."[2] Simply put, examine the areas of your life where you find yourself experiencing the same miserable feeling over and over, and then create a personal rule to protect yourself from it.

Dr. Cloud had a drunk neighbor who came over and started griping at him about something insignificant. Instead of engaging in the conversation, Henry interrupted and said, "I am sorry, but I have a rule. I don't talk to people who are intoxicated. Call me tomorrow and I will be glad to discuss this."[3] The rule he established protected him from the misery and uselessness of discussing a matter with someone while they were intoxicated.

Notice, his rule was set toward his own behavior, not as an attempt to control the other person. We can only control our own choices.

Take a moment to think over the last week or two of interactions with your spouse. Are there any points of pain that stand out to you? Follow the misery back to the root and make a note of what caused it. Look for patterns that may have formed. Are there harsh words spoken in the rush of the morning to get out the door? Perhaps it embarrasses you when he tells those stories about you at small group. Take some time to think through habits you have found to be toxic or just "off" in your marriage. Are there things you've found consistently hurtful? Which of these toxins would be worth fighting to remove, in order to protect your marriage? Make a list. We'll spend some time in the next section of the book working on replacing these paralyzing ruts with healthy rhythms.

Another key tool for getting out of ruts? Look at your community. Who we choose to surround ourselves with is crucial. We all need community, a group of like-minded friends with common values working together toward the same goals. Look at your inner circle. Do you want the kind of marriages you see those closest to you pursuing? If I am trying to practice the rhythm of speaking life, for example, specifically toward my spouse, and I'm regularly spending time with friends who constantly cut down and complain about their spouse, it's going to be pretty hard for me not to get sucked into that habit of negativity. Part of moving into a better rhythm is evaluating the friendships that influence my habits toward my spouse.

A great question to ask is, "Do I want what they have?" If the person telling me about their marriage or offering me advice seems to have a healthy marriage I admire, I'm going to pay close attention. But if the advice I'm receiving is coming from a marriage I don't want to emulate, I can choose not to receive it. We don't necessarily need to cut out all friends in unhealthy marriages from our lives completely, but we may need to create some healthy distance and make the conscious choice to spend more time with friends who are pursuing a healthier idea of marriage.

WHEN RHYTHMS BECOME RUTS

CHRIS ———————————————————————

While most of us can identify the main things that are bothering us in our marriage, sometimes we may not be able to pinpoint the patterns. It's important, though, to find the places that you may have developed ruts in your marriage—because only by naming them can you begin changing them. There are a few ways rhythms can become ruts in our marriage.

- *Seasonal Ruts*: rhythms that served us at one time but no longer help us
- *Inherited Ruts*: rhythms we inherited that never helped us
- *Cultural Ruts*: societal norms that simply don't fit us

Seasonal Ruts

Sometimes a rhythm that at one point served us well as a couple can become a rut simply because the season has changed. Habits that cultivate love in our twenties might not work as well when we're in our thirties or forties. It's important to reevaluate our rhythms in each new season.

One example for us is basketball—we've completely had to

eliminate basketball from our lives. Just kidding! When we were young newlyweds, I would go play basketball all day at the gym with buddies, and Jenni was totally cool with that. But as the seasons shifted, and we added more and more (and more) children, activities, and responsibilities to the mix, the reality of me being gone for hours on end every Saturday just wasn't feasible, or kind toward my family.

Now, this doesn't mean that the longer you're married, the more you have to shuck the things in life that bring you joy, but—to leverage the title of Marshall Goldsmith's book—what got you here won't get you there.[4] Remember, no marriage can thrive when our eyes are consistently focused on ourselves. Creating a thriving marriage requires that we shift our eyes from just our own well-being and happiness to consider our spouse's, as well.

Can you think of habits that used to work in your marriage that now have begun to cause friction? Perhaps it's all-day golf outings, frequent weekend getaways with friends, late nights playing video games—you can fill in the blank. A thriving marriage can't stay stagnant. We have to shift our time and priorities to match the new realities of our ever-changing life. Finding new rhythms for new seasons is not the end of passions and fun, it's just a reorganizing of our world to make sure that the most important people in our life, our spouse and kids, are getting the very best of our energy, time, and attention.

Inherited Rhythms

JENNI ───

When we enter marriage, we each bring our own hefty bag of rhythms, both learned and inherited from our families of origin. But becoming a new family means we get to decide which rhythms we want to keep and which we don't. Some of our inherited habits may be healthy and helpful rhythms, and some may be completely dysfunctional or simply not a good fit for who we are as a couple. The good news is, we get to decide what we will choose to carry on and what we need to let go of.

Depending on your personality, you may fall more naturally to one side than the other. Some of us have a harder time finding any rhythms at all worth repeating. We are tempted to lump our entire bag of inherited rhythms into the category of ruts. Others of us have a hard time seeing any inherited habits as potentially harmful ruts to avoid. What I have found, however, is that no matter the family you come from, if you look hard enough, there are always at least a few good rhythms to hold on to with gratitude and always at least a rut or two that need letting go.

As you think through and discuss with your spouse the inherited habits you learned and received from your own parents, be as kind as you can. Remember, just like you and your spouse, your parents are each children of God, with inherent dignity and value, no matter what example of marriage they gave you growing up. Resist the urge to either completely condemn or entirely glorify whatever set of inherited habits you bring to the table.

One of the inherited rhythms my parents modeled so well for me was the rhythm of generosity. They are just two of the kindest, most servant-hearted people you will ever meet. There is nothing they won't do to help someone God brings across their path. And I believe the Lord has always blessed them greatly because He knows they will be incredible stewards of whatever He gives them.

Growing up, it was pretty impossible to go more than a week in our house without my mom cooking someone a meal, bringing someone a gift, or simply offering a listening ear. I've heard story after story of my dad sending a secret check to help someone in our community who had fallen on hard times, or offering to fix whatever had broken in someone's house around town. If you dropped by their house today, my mom would have some kind of freshly baked good in your hand before you knew it, while my dad would offer to give you a ride on his four-wheeler. Serving is just who they are, and how they live. Chris and I have always been so inspired by that. We want to live out that rhythm too.

One of the inherited ruts Chris and I encountered pretty early on in our marriage was how we handled conflict. My family just fought *loud*. Chris's did not. So, when conflict came, I would instinctively get loud, and Chris would not. Have you ever tried to yell at someone who just isn't yelling back? It's actually quite impossible. If you're the only one yelling, you eventually just begin to look silly. After a while, I remember asking, "Why don't you ever get loud? Don't you have strong feelings?" Turns out, he did have strong feelings—he just didn't feel the need to shout them. Simple as it sounds, that was a huge light bulb moment for me. Over time, I learned how to share my strong feelings without getting loud as well. But it wasn't an easy habit to break.

> You get to chart your own path for your marriage and your life.

In one of our favorite interviews, the late Janice Peterson

shared the key to her long (over sixty years!), happy marriage to her sweetheart, Eugene:

> My mother and father demonstrated love for each other very, very much. They just . . . they *loved* each other; they were *in love* with each other. And Daddy and Mother gave us such a solid base to work out of and to know that—that's what we want! We want to live a good life; we want to have a good marriage. . . . You can't underestimate the amount of influence [family] has on your life.[5]

No matter what your home life was like growing up—whether your parents were crazy about each other or drove each other crazy—the good news is, you get to chart your own path for your marriage and your life. If you were handed unhealthy ruts, you don't have to just continue living them out. You can be the one to stand in the gap for your family and forge a different way forward.

Cultural Ruts

Depending on our personality type, some of us care more about cultural pressure and keeping others around us happy than others do. Usually in marriage, but not always, we fall on opposite ends of the spectrum. This has certainly been true of Chris and me. Chris could generally care less what other people think of him, or whether they are pleased by his choices. But I—though God has grown me a lot in this area—am usually completely aware of the expectations of others, both real and imagined, whether I choose to comply with them or not.

This usually shows up in our marriage in the form of "shoulds." Jordan and Jenna wake up at 5:00 a.m. every morning and work out together. We probably should too. Nate and Kelly have lived in the same house for their entire marriage; we probably should stay put too. John and Amy took their family to Disney World this year, and it looked like they had a blast; we probably should too.

Let me promise you, this is a rut. Now, don't hear what we're not saying. Learning from the habits and values of wise people around us is a vital part of growing; in fact, it's a huge part of what inspired us to write this book. But feeling pressured to adopt other people's rhythms that simply don't fit us is not healthy, and it will not lead to a thriving marriage. This is not how we learn from others. When we strain our marriages to practice rhythms that just don't fit who we are, in order to fall in line with the cultural expectations, keep up with the Joneses, or simply because we think we *should*, we're heading for a rut.

Last year, Chris and I gave in to the cultural pressure to do what many couples do when they have kids—at some point, if it's an option, you have to take them to Disney World, right? I felt a pit in the bottom of my stomach the minute the conversation began. "I think we *have* to go, right?" Chris said with a sigh, as we discussed vacation plans over our morning coffee, both clearly wrestling over our lack of desire to spend an arm and a leg on a crowded theme park. Chris's company was generously offering to cover the flights for our entire family, and a family friend of a friend of a friend got us a substantial discount on park tickets.

"What kind of parents would we be, though, if we never took our kids to Disney World?" Chris joked, and we laughed at the obvious absurdity of the question, while also feeling that we "should" probably take advantage of the opportunity, right? There's that "should" again. Everyone else loves Disney World. We "should" too. Everyone else's Instagram photos confirm that surely it must be the happiest place on earth.

So we gave in. *You only live once*, we thought. Now, before I go on, please let me take a moment and speak to all the Disney-loving readers out there. Listen: We love you, we have nothing at all against the Magic Kingdom, or Dole Whip, or life-size cartoon characters. We are simply sharing an example of what fits and does not fit us as a couple and a family. If theme parks are your thing, that is awesome! Please feel completely free to enjoy the heck out of it. Live it up. Savor each bite of the Mickey Mouse pancakes, sing your heart out at your favorite Disney sing-alongs, stroll through Cinderella's castle. To each his own. For us, however, it was not a world of laughter—it was a world of tears.

We spent an entire February day, from morning to nightfall, running around this overly crowded, freezing theme park, trying our best to make darn sure everyone had as much fun as we spent on this crazy place—feasting ourselves on "nutritious" theme-park food, standing in line after line for rides and shows and activities. By the end of the day, all I could think about was getting the heck out of there.

As we made our way to the exit—make that the line for the tram to the shuttle to the exit—along with the quarter-million other park visitors that day, I noticed something in the faces of some of the other parents we passed. They looked completely miserable.

I watched as some of them tried their best to balance a kid

or two hanging off each arm, wailing and flailing from utter exhaustion, too much candy, too many spins on the teacups, and simply too much overstimulation. One parent actually said out loud to us as we passed each other on the exit ramp, "How much did we pay for this?" Many of us seemed to be asking ourselves the same question.

No one looked particularly refreshed and rejuvenated, filled with gratitude and wonder at the golden moments they'd enjoyed as a family. Our family was ready to drop, dreaming of our nice warm beds and cozy blankets. We weren't feeling the kind of tired-but-full you hope to feel after a day together in a magical place. We felt empty and exhausted.

After we traveled the many miles back to our hotel room, got the kids all tucked in tight, and finally collapsed in the beds we'd been dreaming of all day, Chris and I looked at each other and said, with weary eyes half open, "Let's never do that again, okay?" Some lessons you have to learn the hard way.

We thought of all the other incredible things we could have possibly done with the money we spent on that day. Breathtaking mountains and rivers we could have enjoyed. Refreshing time spent splashing in the ocean, fishing at the lake, or camping out together, underneath the majestic stars. How different would we have felt after time spent where we truly wanted to be?

But we did receive a valuable gift that day. We found the misery and made a rule. And it has informed every trip we've planned ever since. We are not theme-park people, and that is okay. We feel no need to prove otherwise. We now try our best to intentionally choose activities and places that will speak to who *we* are as a family, to vacations we *actually* enjoy, not the ones the world tells us we *should* enjoy.

THE NEW HAS COME

Take hold of the life that is truly life.

1 TIMOTHY 6:19

I recently spent time sorting through some boxes of old pictures for my parents—and wow. Seeing your life flash before your eyes sure has a way of opening them. As I flipped through photo after photo, looking across my journey through pictures, I realized I spent a lot of time trying things on that just didn't fit me. I'm not referring only to those tight pleather pants or that crop-top phase I went through (although, yes, those definitely did not fit). I spent a lot of years trying to live out a script I thought everyone around me wanted me to live. Striving. Pushing. Stressing. Trying feverishly to be someone I was not. To make things fit that just were not meant to. Relationships. Majors. Careers. Identities.

And then, Jesus. When I encountered Jesus, He set me free from all of it. Not only did He set me free, He actually gave me a *new* identity. He took hold of my empty hand and led me into a life that truly did fit. Step-by-step, as I laid down every piece of my life that did not work, did not fit, He so graciously replaced it with something new that fit like a glove. Every single "no" He enabled me to say to the old, He faithfully replaced with a "yes" to the new, more beautiful life He had for me. This is what He does.

> Therefore, if anyone is in Christ, he is a new creation.
> The old has passed away; behold, the new has come.
> 2 CORINTHIANS 5:17, ESV

Look across your life for a moment. Are there rhythms you've been eagerly trying to adopt that just don't fit? As one of my favorite James Taylor songs says, "You can play the game, you can act out the part, though you know it wasn't written for you."[6] It can be really hard to give up the rhythms that *almost* work. But here's what I know: The counterfeits we cling to don't hold a candle to the life God has for us. His ways are so much higher than ours. Whenever He asks us to let go of something, it is *always* so that He can replace it with something inconceivably better.

Have you noticed any places or patterns where you feel miserable and stuck but have just settled in? Do you sense somewhere deep down that there's *more* God has for you and for your marriage? Right where you are, take a moment. Ask God to open your eyes to any rhythms that have become ruts. As He begins to identify anything you've been trying to make fit that clearly is not from Him, take a moment to lay it at His feet. Surrender is such a beautiful gift. You are not stuck. We are not stuck. Life and marriage are ours for the changing.

So let's remove the obstacles and clear the way. Rebuild the road, inch by inch, rhythm by rhythm, to the life you long for, the thriving relationship He has for you. Say no to something you know is not working, today. Remove the ruts. Make way for the best rhythms. Say yes to something new and beautiful. The no we say today makes way for the yes in our future.

PRACTICE

- Spend some time with your spouse this week and ask each other, "Where do we feel out of rhythm?"

- Take a moment and make a list of what *is* working. What areas immediately come to mind as you think of being *in* rhythm with each other?

- What comes to mind when you think of wonderful rhythms you inherited from your family of origin?

- Which inherited rhythms have become more of a rut for your marriage?

- Take a moment and make a list of what's not working in your marriage. What rhythms have become ruts?

PART TWO

THE
CORE RHYTHMS

A GREAT MARRIAGE UNFOLDS in endless ways, and we could not possibly attempt to write an exhaustive book that includes absolutely every aspect. But every marriage needs a starting point, a few attainable rhythms that lay the groundwork for all the rest. These five core rhythms are those we have learned from thriving couples in our own lives, the same rhythms that have carried us through seventeen years of marriage.

We encourage you to take notice of the couples God has placed in your life, the people you can learn from. In the back of the book, we've carved out some space for you to do just that, to consider and jot down the way these rhythms come to life in the people around you and the ways they might come to life for you.

Friends, we hope and pray as you dive into these five rhythms that you won't be able to get them out of your head. That as you go about your day, they will stay with you, and that as you begin to practice them, they will take you step-by-step, choice by choice, closer and closer to the life and marriage you truly long for.

4

WORDS MATTER

The Rhythm of Speaking Life

Death and life are in the power of the tongue.

PROVERBS 18:21, ESV

Words create. God's Word creates. Our words
can participate in the creation.

EUGENE PETERSON

JENNI

Some of my favorite memories from growing up are the family trips we took every fall to the beautiful Texas Hill Country with a few other close friends. After a scorching-hot Texas summer, the wonderful cool breeze and crisp golden leaves of autumn were always an event worth celebrating. At meals, the adults would all gather at one end of the table and all the rowdy kids would congregate at the other. Being the obsessive observer of relationships that I was, I always loved quietly scooting as close as I could to listen in on the adult conversations. Almost every night, without fail, as the meal wound down, the dialogue would ultimately turn to teasing as each couple took turns telling jokes about each other. It seemed playful at first, but eventually you could start to hear the tension behind the banter: "Listen to what this bozo did last week." "You wouldn't believe what Sara said last night!"

There was one couple, however, who always stood out to me: Mike and Linda. They just never joined in the game. In fact, it was clear how much they seemed to genuinely enjoy each other, and the only fun stories they would offer to the group revealed just how much they truly adored each other. Something about their relationship struck me, and deep down, I made one of my mental notes for my future marriage: *Never throw your spouse under the bus.*

Years later, when Chris and I met, fell in love, and got engaged, I remembered Mike and Linda's thriving marriage and decided it would be a good idea to learn from the best. So we packed up our bags and took a trip down to Birmingham to spend a weekend learning from this incredible couple. It was one of the sweetest gifts God gave us as we began our life together. Each night, we let the candles burn all the way to the bottom as we sipped our French roast and soaked up every drop of wisdom we could from these two sweet sages on what it means to love each other well for a lifetime.

> Never throw your spouse under the bus.

One of the greatest lessons they taught us was the very principle that had caught my attention all those years ago over Texas BBQ: Never throw your spouse under the bus. Or, to put it another way: Always speak life over your spouse.

As it turns out, this principle is straight out of God's Word: "Death and life are in the power of the tongue, and those who love it will eat its fruits" (Proverbs 18:21, ESV). That winter weekend, Mike and Linda unpacked a truth we have seen confirmed over and over in our own marriage and in countless thriving couples we've encountered along the way: The words we speak over each other literally have the potential to create and build life in us . . . or to poison and destroy us. **Thriving couples choose to speak words of life over each other.**

Words matter. What a powerful gift we've been given, one that requires incredible stewardship. We possess the power to shape our spouse's sense of identity, for better or worse, with our words. We get to contribute to the shaping of who they are becoming. Every day we wake up next to each other, we can choose to see the good and speak it out loud, or we can focus on their faults and point them out every chance we get. Either way, as Portland pastor John Mark Comer says, "They will rise or fall to meet the expectations we place on them."[1]

Comer continues, "When we show honor to others, we open ourselves up to receive from all they have to give, but when we dishonor them, we cut ourselves off from all that they are and all that they carry."[2] Each human we encounter, including our spouse, is a child of God—a walking, talking miracle, full of unique gifts, strengths, and abilities to be discovered.

When we honor our spouse with our words, we open our lives up to share in the extraordinary gift of who they are. And when we cut them down with words of dishonor, not only do we poison them with our disrespect but we also miss out on the blessing and the beauty that they carry.

Think of the couples you admire most in your life. One thing we've noticed, time and time again, is that any thriving couple who has made it together over the long haul has this way of talking about each other with a deep sense of admiration and respect. Take it to the bank. This foundational sense of deep respect simply must be present in order for a couple to thrive. Even in moments of conflict and frustration, the couple remains strong and leans on this underlying sense of appreciation. It's almost like a safety net.

To thrive, we have to respect each other as people. One of the things that sealed the deal for me with Chris (even before we started dating, when we were just friends) was how respected I felt by him—more than anyone I've ever met. I would overhear him from time to time in a conversation with a friend, quoting something I had said. "Yeah man, I was talking to Jenni the other day, and she said x, y, and z. It was so good." Or "Yeah, Jenni taught me this thing about prayer, I can't stop thinking about . . ." He just had this way of always noticing the absolute best in me and holding it up like a trophy for the world to see. He saw things that I couldn't even see in myself.

Are there negative behaviors in a relationship that need addressing? Of course. But even in our honesty, we can still choose to speak to each other with words of kindness, viewing even our hard conversations as an opportunity to build one another up. You'll be surprised at the positive results you see in your spouse when you simply shift to pointing out their strengths rather than their faults, reminding them of who they really are. According to Dr. John Gottman, "People can change only if they feel that they are basically liked and accepted the way they are. When people feel criticized, disliked, and unappreciated they are unable to change. Instead, they feel under siege and dig in to protect themselves."[3]

There's a reason why we began with this particular rhythm. We truly believe it has the greatest potential for change and is the foundation for all the other rhythms because the words we speak toward each other create the culture between us. If the environment of our relationship is filled with words of criticism and contempt, no amount of romantic gestures will make a dent of difference. But we hold the power to change the environment of our relationship—simply by changing our words.

AFFIRM THE GOOD

So, what are some practical ways we can begin to grow in this rhythm? Here's the easiest place to begin: When you think something nice, say it out loud. This sounds very simple, I know—but it's often the simplest things that can make the biggest difference.

I realize this practice will be easier for some than others. When we first got married, this rhythm of speaking life did not come naturally to me at all. The family I grew up in was very loving and wonderful, but our idea of affirming each other looked more like sarcasm and banter than audible words of encouragement. It wasn't that we didn't think plenty of nice things about each other; we just didn't speak them out loud on a regular basis. As it turns out, the power is not just in thinking well of another but in speaking those things out loud.

Over time, however, as I saw how important it was to Chris (and how easy it was for him to affirm those around him), this rhythm began to rub off on me. Just like everything else in life worth pursuing, speaking life takes practice. Give yourself plenty of grace and time, but just begin. When you think something nice, say it out loud. Awkward as it may be at first, just give it a try, and then another, and another. And over

> The power is not just in thinking well of another but in speaking those things out loud.

time, your spouse will begin to hold their head higher and even grow stronger in the areas you take the time to intentionally acknowledge and affirm.

When he does the dishes, even if it's not the way you would like them done, thank him and affirm his thoughtfulness. When she musters up the courage to try something new, even if she's wobbly at first, shower her with praise for the grit and guts it takes to tackle a new skill. There will always be plenty of good to affirm and plenty of faults to criticize. The choice is ours. What will we choose to acknowledge and affirm? Remember, with each blessing we speak, we're contributing to the reality of the person they're becoming.

And *we* become someone new, as well. As we practice the habit of looking for the good and speaking it out loud, not only are we participating in the transformation of those we love—we ourselves are changed. We become people whose eyes have been trained to see the good and to make much of it. To let compassion and mercy be our guide, remembering we are all flawed human beings on a journey. No one has arrived. Look for the *good* and say it out loud.

AFFIRM THE GIFT
CHRIS

Speaking words of life goes to this whole new level when we ask God to help us notice and name the gifts and callings God has given our spouse. No one knows them better than you do, and no one's opinion matters more than yours. We both entered our marriage as a whole person, with dreams, gifts, and abilities. Part of a healthy, thriving marriage is acknowledging, nurturing, and prioritizing our spouse's gifts, as well as our own. Look for their talents, abilities, and passions; encourage your spouse in those things; and watch them come to life.

Our words aren't the only important thing—our time and resources help affirm what we see in our spouse. If she's really into crafts, surprise her with a gift card to Michaels or carve out a small space in your home for her to get her craft on in the house. If he's really good at photography, help him get a website up or put a portfolio together. Maybe she comes alive when she's writing. Surprise her with a few hours all to herself at her favorite coffee shop, to dream and write. The sky is the limit.

When we get the opportunity to see someone we love doing what *they* love, we fall in love with them all over again. Research shows that we are most attracted to our spouse when we see them doing something they enjoy and are good at. Popular marriage expert Esther Perel did a survey on what attracts people back to their partner in long-term relationships, and this is what she found:

> There are a few answers that just keep coming back . . .
> I am most drawn to my partner when I see him in
> the studio, when she is onstage, when he is in his
> element, when she's doing something she's passionate
> about . . . Basically, when I look at my partner radiant
> and confident—probably the biggest turn-on across
> the board.[4]

When we take the time to notice and name what makes our spouse come alive, *we* actually are blessed too. Thriving couples cheer each other on and give each other freedom to spread their wings.

AFFIRM THE TRUTH
JENNI

One of the things we hear most from friends struggling in their marriage is, "I just wish I could change *x*, *y*, or *z* about my spouse." But here's the truth about a thriving marriage: The greatest thing you can do to change your spouse is to affirm who they truly are. I'm not saying you affirm how they may be acting in this current season, or behaviors that may be harmful—but rather *the person you know God has truly created them to be*. What a beautiful gift we can give to each other.

Thriving couples know who their spouse truly is, and they will always question the circumstances contributing to their spouse's behavior before they question the character of their spouse. When life tries to pull us away from that person we're meant to be, we can remind each other of our true identity in Christ. Thriving couples speak the truth in love.

One of my favorite Scriptures is 1 Corinthians 5:7: "Get rid of the old yeast, so that you may be a new unleavened batch—as you really are." *As you really are*. It's easy to size ourselves and others up by the total sum of our faults, but the truth is, that's not who we really are. According to God's Word, if we are in Christ, we have been made new—not because of how perfectly we behaved today but because of His sacrifice that covers us. So, the old me, though she may show up from time to time, is not who I really am. I have been given a brand-new identity in Christ. I am covered by the sacrifice of my Savior and made new in Him.[5] What a gift, when my spouse, the most powerful voice in my life, can be the one to remind me.

Does that mean that we should avoid all conflict in our

> Thriving couples speak the truth in love.

marriage or ignore harmful issues that bother us? Of course not. Part of loving someone well and speaking to the best of who they are will include being honest when conflict arises. And there isn't a couple alive who doesn't experience conflict. A healthy part of any marriage is having the freedom and trust to bring what bothers you out into the light where you and your spouse can deal with it appropriately. The key is to still speak to each other in a tone that is loving and kind, while also being open and honest about where we've been hurt. If we speak the truth in a way that belittles, accuses, or devalues our spouse, our words will be counterproductive.

Maturity in life and in marriage means being able to separate the person we love from the issue we don't.

When tackling conflict in our marriage, it's important that we speak to the problem, rather than make our *spouse* the problem. If we successfully communicate how we honestly feel yet use a tone and harshness that destroys the person and the relationship in the process, we will have failed. The *way* we speak matters. If we aren't careful, even when our feelings about our spouse's actions are justified, the hurtful way in which we communicate our honest feelings can cause more harm than the actual issue itself.

Dr. Henry Cloud advises, "Be hard on the issue, but soft on the person."[6] Maturity in life and in marriage means being able to separate the person we love from the issue we don't. And although I know it's not easy, sharing openly about what's bothering you with a heart of love and kindness will produce far better results than harsh words of truth ever will. As Martin Luther King Jr. said, "Darkness cannot drive out darkness; only light can do that. Hate cannot drive out hate; only love can do that."[7]

BE *FOR* YOUR SPOUSE

Thriving couples are *for* each other. When you truly believe that the people around you are *for* you, something within you relaxes. You hold your head a little higher and start acting like the person you truly are.

Nothing poisons a relationship like comparison and competition. There is just no room for it in a healthy marriage. We are both on a journey of transformation in Christ, a path to becoming more and more like Him. Neither one of us has arrived. And our job on that journey is not to compete with each other, but to become each other's loudest supporters. No relationship can thrive when we're constantly competing with one another. There is no winner in that game.

> Thriving couples are *for* each other.

In seasons of hardship, we can dignify our spouse with words of gratitude for their efforts and speak encouragement and hope for their future. In seasons of fear, we can cling to each other with words of trust, rather than turn on each other with words of accusation. In seasons of great joy and celebration, we can offer words of praise and thankfulness, knowing the only true Source of so much life. We create the reality we desire with the words we choose to speak.

The rhythm of speaking life will become easier and easier the more you engage it. If we say "I love you" only when we feel like it, it won't happen often enough. If I think nice things but never say them out loud, they don't actually count. But as we experience the benefit of good words, and as we practice speaking words of life toward our spouse, we'll start to see the impact it makes on each other and on our connection. Start with a simple, daily practice, and over time, it will begin to flow more naturally.

I also want to acknowledge that there are times in a relationship when it's hard to find anything at all you feel is worth praising or affirming. Maybe you feel stuck in a cycle of hurtful words and actions. Friend, pray for what you lack (James 1:5). Pause for a moment now and ask the Lord to reveal the good in your spouse, to help you remember who they truly are. Ask Him to open your eyes to see them as He does, and then start to treat them as if they already were all those things you know they can be. It's amazing what happens when someone believes in us and speaks to us with that kind of honor and respect. Everything inside us wants to rise to become the extraordinary person they believe us to be.

> Sometimes all it takes is one word of love to reverse the cycle of unkindness.

Give it a try. Watch what God will do. Sometimes all it takes is one word of love to reverse the cycle of unkindness. You could be the one to change it all. And right there, from one moment of kindness, the healing begins.

PRACTICE

- Pray for eyes to see where you can affirm the good you notice in your spouse, and for the courage to say it out loud.

- Affirming the good can be difficult, especially if you did not grow up hearing others model it. Start with writing a small note of prayer or encouragement on a particularly stressful or important day, or by giving a simple compliment.

- Praise your spouse in public this week (in front of actual humans, not on social media). Find something you can genuinely affirm in them, and then affirm it in a sincere way in front of your friends or family. Watch them lift their head a little higher.

- What is your spouse good at? What have you seen them light up talking about? Affirm it in them this week. Find a tangible way to make space for them to grow in it.

- Spend some time with the Lord this week, asking Him to change the way you see your spouse to the way He does and to help you treat them accordingly.

- Is there an area of conflict with your spouse where you find yourself continually tempted to speak harshly? What would it look like for you to speak openly and honestly about how you feel without accusing, belittling, or devaluing them as a child of God?

5

TEAM US

The Rhythm of Serving

There are no **ordinary** people. You have never talked to a mere mortal.

C. S. LEWIS

The greatest among you will be your servant.

MATTHEW 23:11

Linda wakes up each morning to the clink of the cup on the plate as Michael lovingly sets her morning coffee on their side table. As she sips, they read a bit of Scripture together, say a prayer for their day, and launch into the rest of their morning. This little ritual of serving each other with a morning cup of coffee and a little time of prayer has been their daily rhythm for over thirty years.[1]

For decades, Kate never had to touch a gas pump. John kept her tank full every week, just as a simple way to show how much he valued her and wanted to take extra-good care of her. "Look at her—she's so beautiful! Those hands should never have to touch a gas pump," was his response when asked about their little weekly practice. By simply keeping her gas tank full each week, he communicated how precious she was to him and how much he valued caring for her.

One of the simple, everyday ways Jenni has blessed me ever since we first got married is by tackling the laundry. Now, it's not that I'm not capable—I'll have you know. My mom made dang sure I was doing my own laundry by the age of eight, long before I was even tall enough to reach those knobs on our old-school, yellow washer and dryer. But laundry has always been one of those chores that falls to the very bottom of the list for me, and honestly, if I were in charge of the sifting and sorting of all the whites, colors, socks, and undies in our current home of seven, it would be a total disaster. But for Jenni, laundry is something she just doesn't mind doing, and because she worked her way through college at many a retail store, she's quite skilled at the fluffing and folding of it all.

For Jenni, it's dishes. With five kids, you can imagine just how quickly our kitchen sink can turn into a hot mess of food-covered plates and who knows what else. Play-Doh, socks, toothpicks, you name it—we've seen it all! My beautiful wife doesn't particularly enjoy sticking her hand into that melting pot of gross. But back in the day, I worked in the restaurant world for years and have plenty of experience grabbing a plate from a table to find my thumb buried in some stranger's mashed potatoes. It doesn't bother me one bit. So, most of the time, I tackle the dishes.

These are simple, everyday examples, but they matter. Serving your spouse doesn't have to be complicated or fancy. It's the choice to love through serving that matters. A small gesture communicates volumes of care and thoughtfulness. When I open my underwear drawer to find it's been magically replenished, or when Jenni comes around the corner to find the sink empty and the counters wiped down, it's money in the bank for our relationship. Sure, we can choose to see these acts as "our responsibility"—or we can choose to see them as a gift we can give to each other. A simple act of serving is a way to say I love you at a whole new level. Thriving couples intentionally serve each other.

One of the greatest gifts we were given at the very beginning of our marriage was the opportunity to sit with and learn from a handful of inspiring, remarkable couples whom we greatly admired, as they graciously poured out their wisdom for us young bucks. One of the rhythms we found to be true of each of these couples and that continues to be true of thriving couples we meet along the way is the intentional way they *serve* one another. It seems to be a keystone value that's held across the board. Think for a moment of the couples you admire most, and I promise you, if you were to map out their weekly rhythms, focusing on each other's needs would rise to the top of the list.

> Thriving couples intentionally serve each other.

Of course, most of us wake up each morning thinking of our own needs first, almost involuntarily. *I sure need some coffee . . . Whew! I've got that meeting coming up today . . . Man, my muscles are tight; I sure could use a massage . . .* We just wake up immediately aware of our own needs and our own agenda. As Jan Peterson said, "We all start out self-centered . . . Our wants are our world."[2] It takes a great deal of practice and considerable intention to train our eyes to see in a different way, but no marriage can flourish when our eyes are consistently focused on ourselves.

In fact, a life focused only on ourselves is no life at all. As a good pastor friend of ours says, "People interested only in themselves will have the most difficulty in life and cause the most danger for others."[3] People who consistently choose to show genuine interest in those around them are rare and magnetic. We gravitate toward them. If a marriage only serves one person, it will start to fall apart. We have to intentionally shift our eyes, choose to see, care about, and get to know our spouse's world as well as our own. Thriving couples are thoroughly interested in each other's lives.

> Marriage is not for the weak, the selfish, the insecure.
> TO SIR, WITH LOVE

WHAT SERVING LOOKS LIKE

Removing ourselves from the center of our universe and stepping into the rhythm of serving not only brings tremendous joy to our spouse—we receive great benefit, as well. As poet Maya Angelou said, "You shouldn't go through life with a catcher's mitt on both hands; you need to be able to throw something back."[4] As we grow toward maturity in life and in marriage, strengthening our ability to see beyond our own wants and needs, we find that "throwing something back" is actually a lot of fun. In fact, it's one of the greatest joys in life! When we go out of our way to make someone else happy, the joy becomes our own. When was the last time you went out of your way to serve your spouse and watched their face light up with joy? There's nothing like it.

Now, you may be thinking of all the times you've served your spouse—picking up the kids from school, doing the grocery shopping, taking the dog out at three in the morning—and felt like the act went unnoticed. There were no signs of joy, no giddy reactions toward your amazing acts of kindness. Moments like that don't feel good. We want our work to be seen, our intentions noticed and affirmed. But the rhythm of serving really isn't about the high fives we get on the other side. Hearing a "thank you" or getting a nice hug and kiss are sweet bonuses, but, at the end of the day, serving our spouse is more about the transformation of our own heart rather than the praise we receive.

One of the most powerful stories of serving in the Scriptures is when Jesus was hours away from experiencing His brutal death on the cross. In that moment, in the upper room with His disciples, it would have been easy for Him to desire praise and affirmation as He looked toward what He was about to face. But what did He do instead? He served. He wrapped a towel around His waist, took the lowliest position He could, and went from person to person, washing their dirty, stinky feet (John 13:1-17).

We look most like our Savior when we choose to serve others. We don't serve because it's easy or because of what we might receive in return. We serve because this is the rhythm modeled for us by the One we follow. Now, I'm not saying that washing your husband's sweaty gym clothes or sticking your hand in a sink full of disgusting, swampy dishwater is the same as Jesus washing the disciple's feet. But we can posture ourselves with the same heart that Jesus had on that incredible night—the heart of a servant. Resist the urge to keep score. Serve without expectation of return. Throw away the scorecard, and trust God to take care of you.

Our motive in serving our spouse shouldn't be about what
we get in return. It should always be *lending strength*. This may
be particularly important if you happen to be married to someone who resists being served and prefers to be completely self-
sufficient or independent. (I may or may not be speaking from
experience here.) Honestly, after seventeen years of marriage, we
are still working on this one. The fact that Jenni
and I are both so independent and strong-willed
was one of the very first things that attracted us
to each other. Strength is one of the highest core
values we share. So *needing* each other is something we've always had to work on. Enjoying
each other comes naturally for us. *Needing* one
another, *leaning* on each other? Not as much. But the truth is,
we truly do need one another, and if we're not careful, we can
spend all our best energy serving everyone else around us with
more obvious needs and unintentionally be left with only scraps
to piece together at the end of the day for one another.

> Throw away the scorecard, and trust God to take care of you.

Remember, thriving couples are *for* each other, not against.
When we choose intentional ways to look outside ourselves and
see our spouse, see what they really need, serving becomes the
lifeblood of our marriage.

> Let each one give as he purposes in his heart, not
> grudgingly or of necessity; for God loves a cheerful giver.
> 2 CORINTHIANS 9:7, NKJV

Enter Their World

Learning how to shift the focus off ourselves and toward serving
each other is not an easy task. It's an ongoing process. Early on

in marriage, the concept of consistently and intentionally serving the other person can seem so foreign. We've lived our own independent lives and done our own thing for so many years, then suddenly two become one, and it's "die to yourself" time. It can be difficult, laying down our own needs, desires, and agenda to consider those of another, even someone we dearly love. But what we have discovered is that as it becomes a part of our life rhythm, choosing to see and meet our spouse where they're at and serve them there is where the greatest joy is found.

When we were first married, we decided Jenni staying at home while our kids were little was a nonnegotiable rhythm for us. Though it was something we both truly wanted, this rhythm still took some major adjusting for both of us. My work took us all over the place—Tennessee, California, North Carolina, and Texas. (Jenni knew she was signing up for an adventure when she married me!) But during this season, she chose to serve our family by surrendering her dreams and desires so that she could be at home with our little ones, while they were still little.

During that season, God opened my eyes to see how I could serve her by entering her world and noticing how exhausted she was by the end of the week. I knew she loved being at home with the kids, but it was also very clear that come Thursday, she needed a little time to herself to refresh and recharge. I decided that every Friday, I would work from home so Jenni could have a few hours all to herself. Little did we all realize how much this was needed—not just for Jenni, but for our entire family.

We all need our own space. To this day, I still (lovingly) kick her out of the house every Friday, and she always comes back feeling refreshed and alive, ready to jump back into enjoying our family. In fact, one of my favorite parts of the week is the text I get from Jenni on Fridays when she's off filling her tank, usually walking through some kind of forest, saying how much she loves me and how grateful she is for that time to recharge. And it fills my tank too.

Entering someone's world, thinking of their needs, and meeting those needs in creative ways doesn't come naturally to most of us. But at the core of any thriving marriage are two people who pay attention to the other person's world and choose to meet specific needs there.

> Love others as you love yourself. That's an act of true
> freedom.
> GALATIANS 5:14, MSG

This is where the journey gets really personal. Each couple is unique, and the meaningful ways in which you can serve your spouse will look radically different from how Jenni and I serve each other. This rhythm of serving requires getting to know your spouse, taking time to truly listen to their lives and enter their world. What do they love? Where could they use a break? When is the last time you gave them your full, undistracted attention? Asked about *their* dreams? *Their* loves? *Their* spiritual journey? It is virtually impossible to love the people around us well if we care nothing for their world and their loves. Serving our spouse builds a bridge from our life to theirs. We love them by entering their world.

Serving our spouse builds a bridge from our life to theirs. We love them by entering their world.

Those who exalt themselves will be humbled, and
those who humble themselves will be exalted.

MATTHEW 23:12

See Truly

Put aside any frustrations that you may have with your spouse,
just for a moment (you can pull them out again later). But for
now, just for this moment, let yourself be reminded that this
extraordinary, made-in-the-image-of-God human being right
in front of you is one of the greatest gifts God
has ever given you. The opportunity to know
and love another is a *miracle*. Ask God to give
you fresh eyes to see your spouse for the miracle
he or she is. Who has He created them to be?
As we discussed earlier, change always begins
with honesty and repentance. If He leads you to, perhaps take
this time to acknowledge and surrender ways you've come to
view your spouse as less than, or without inherent value and
dignity, and treated them accordingly.

The opportunity to know and love another is a miracle.

As the saying goes, "Familiarity breeds contempt." Contempt
is one of the greatest predictors of divorce.[5] Contempt occurs
when we allow ourselves to focus so habitually on the faults of
another that in our minds, that person becomes the problem.
Ask God to enable you to see the good, to see your spouse
as He does. Just like you and I, they are not the sum of their
faults. And they do not belong to you, in fact, but rather have
been *entrusted* to you as a gift to love and to care for. Loving
our spouse well begins with shifting our perspective to view
them as a remarkable gift to treasure rather than a heavy burden to bear.

Give, and you will receive. You will be given much.
Pressed down, shaken together, and running over, it
will spill into your lap. The way you give to others
is the way God will give to you.

LUKE 6:38, NCV

When I break out of my self-absorption and see my spouse
as the remarkable person they truly are, created in the image
of God, suddenly I am motivated to soak up every moment
I've been given with them. Each day becomes a gift. I am now
enabled to see with fresh eyes the ways I can put their well-
being above my own, ways I can serve, care for, and bless them.
But the first step is entering their world. What do they love?
What makes them come alive? What do they dream of doing?
How can I help them make those dreams a reality? As theologian and pastor Tim Keller says, "Serving your spouse . . .
means showing that you are committed to his or her well-
being and flourishing. This kind of love is given when you
seek to help your spouse develop gifts and pursue aspirations
for growth."[6] Not only will serving your spouse in this way
restore the bond you have together, it will also renew your
own joy as you experience the pleasure of helping someone else
and watching them grow and flourish. There's nothing like it.
Give it a try.

Empty Yourself

JENNI ─────────────────────────────────────

When the kids are all finally tucked in tight, and I get to cozy
up under my covers with a nice cup of hot tea and a good book
by 8:30 p.m., that's what I call a successful evening! Candle.

Journal. Good book. Bliss. (Yes, I know. I've fully embraced my nerdiness.)

Last night I was reading about negative capability—what Eugene Peterson described as "a noticeable feature in all skilled workers."[7] Whether we're cooking hamburgers, raising a family, or building a marriage, real work, the truly skilled kind, requires this negative capability, this act of emptying ourselves so that the greatest work can take place on its own. All truly great work requires this cultivation of humility; a sense of great respect toward the work itself. "He must increase, but I must decrease" is embedded in all good work (John 3:30, ESV). I glanced over at Chris sleeping soundly next to me, and I thought of our marriage, of this life we are building together, and how the greatest work God wants to do in and through us requires this emptying.

So, before my head hit the pillow, I whispered a quiet prayer for both Chris and me: "Lord, help us empty ourselves, so that Your greatest work can flow freely from us." Within just a few hours, in the middle of the night, Chris and I were suddenly awakened by the sound every parent fears. Whimpering, crying, screaming, gagging, and then—yep, you guessed it—vomiting. Jolted wide awake by the startling sound, we both rushed down the hall to find our sweet youngest daughter covered head to toe in her regurgitated dinner.

We were still both half asleep, struggling to keep our aching eyes open, but thankfully, having been at this parenting thing now for over a decade together, our muscle memory kicked in. We both launched almost automatically into the rhythm of cleanup: stripping sheets, wiping chins, changing pj's . . . just like riding a bike. (Although a little less fun.)

This routine repeated itself three more times over the next few hours of the night. At one point, I was holding Keris's tiny blonde curls back as she threw up for the third time, cradling this sweet babe in my arms, feeling so helpless to stop her pain—and very aware of the pain and exhaustion in my own body. I suddenly remembered the prayer I'd whispered before I fell asleep: "Lord, help us empty ourselves."

It hit me. There we were, right smack in the middle of an opportunity to be emptied. To pour what little energy we had left out for another. To allow God to do the work in and through us, when we were completely empty and had nothing left to give. I looked over at Chris as he sweetly scrubbed the sheets, holding his breath from the smell. He didn't know I had prayed the empty-us prayer on his behalf too. *So this is emptying*, I thought.

I remembered Eugene's words, how the best work, the truly great work can only come as we are emptied. Right there in the middle of the bathroom floor, we were doing the best work. The truly great work. Together. The Lord reminded me in that moment of how often, some of the greatest opportunities for His work to flow freely through us come to us disguised as inconveniences.

Thriving couples we've encountered along the way seem to possess an acute understanding of this "emptying." A cultivation of humility. They understand what it means to pour themselves out in seemingly small moments that add up to a truly great work, a thriving, rich relationship. They've learned somewhere along the way how to rely on the sustaining strength that only comes from the Lord rather than trying to merely scrape by on their own. Each time we pour ourselves out for our spouse, choosing to allow our agenda, our plans to be altered so that we might serve them, we are not only contributing to their joy and well-being but laying brick upon brick to build the thriving marriage we long for. A truly great work. But it is found only on the other side of emptying ourselves.

Listen Well

One of the greatest ways we can serve each other is simply by listening. Years ago, when Chris and I were serving as young college pastors in the Dallas area, someone introduced us to the missional-church movement. We began listening to missional-church leaders such as Michael Frost, Reggie McNeal, and Alan Hirsch, who taught us what it looked like to live on mission in the world around us. Living on mission means shifting our focus from bringing as many people as possible to church on Sunday to learning to see our communities as a mission field, venturing out into our neighborhoods, and being the hands and feet of Jesus to people right where they are.

As pastors, we realized for the first time that maybe it wasn't all about the weekend, after all. Maybe building the Kingdom of God looked less like packing people into our church buildings and more like entering their world, getting to know them right in the middle of their unique lives and circumstances, and showing them the love of Jesus right there.

I'll never forget the conviction I felt hearing that message for the first time. I could not make it through an entire sermon on the topic without ending up on my knees. We had the scorecard wrong. *I* had the scorecard wrong. I wanted to change. I wanted to make a difference in the lives of those around me. I wanted to care more intentionally for each person I encountered, viewing every single one of them as someone with great dignity and value, as someone Jesus loved.

In one of the teachings on repeat in our home and in our circle of friends, Reggie McNeal encouraged us to simply try to bless three people every week. Just bless. Not witness to them, not give them a tract or invite them to church, just find a way to bless them. Now, we were young college pastors with two young kids and a tight budget, leading young college students with limited budgets of their own. None of us had a lot of extra money or resources lying around to use to bless people, so we had to get creative. One of the most surprising yet most meaningful ways we found to bless was something we all had complete access to and could easily afford: *listening*.

> We bestow great dignity and value on a person when we simply take the time to pay attention and listen well.

You would be shocked at the stories that began to roll in of lives in our community that were touched by the simple blessing of a listening ear. It is so rare, as it turns out, to encounter a person who will truly pause what they're doing and offer you their full presence and attention, without agenda. But listening is the single best way we found to reach people in our community. We couldn't believe the stories we heard as lives were touched by the simple blessing of a listening ear. We encouraged our students to just ask someone, "What's your story?" and then listen, offering their full presence as a way of serving. We bestow great dignity and value on a person when we simply take the time to pay attention and listen well.

As we step into the rhythm of serving our spouse, we must

learn how to listen. It's impossible to truly love someone, to serve their deepest needs, unless you get to know them. Taking the time to listen to your spouse communicates desire, conveys respect, and can even restore dignity. When I stop what I'm doing, put away my screen, and take the time to listen to what my spouse needs to share, I am communicating to them, *You are valuable to me, and I care. Your life is worth knowing, worth way more than any distraction vying for my attention right now.*

Feeling heard and understood causes us to feel safe. Empathy has a calming effect. According to psychologist Dr. Henry Cloud, "We can't begin to solve problems until there is a sense of trust, and trust is established when we feel listened to."[8]

Listen to your spouse's words—and listen to their life. Ask God to open your eyes to ways you could serve your spouse that would be particularly meaningful to them. Listen for what they're going through, what they care about, and listen to what they need. Maybe they have a sore ankle from a sprain that happened while running months ago, and serving them looks like picking up a brace from Walgreens and leaving it on their nightstand. Maybe by Thursday, they're completely worn out, and serving them looks like offering to watch the kids while they meet a friend for coffee or just go for a quiet walk through the trees. Serving could even look like stopping to pray for them when they're having a hard day.

When we posture ourselves as a servant toward each other, train our eyes to see in a different way, and take the time to listen to what our spouse truly needs, we develop a rhythm of serving that changes the trajectory of our marriage.

Lend Your Strengths

CHRIS ——————————————————————————————

God has a way of causing opposites to attract. More than likely, one of you is probably an extrovert and one an introvert, one spontaneous and one a planner, or, as Dave Ramsey says, one a "nerd" and the other a "free spirit."[9] When we practice seeing our spouse as a gift, their strengths become a gift to us, as well. Thriving couples serve each other by sharing their strengths. We serve each other by coming alongside, filling in the gaps, and bolstering each other with our strengths. Perhaps the "nerd" of the family gets to offer strength through creating the family budget and helping manage the money. The extrovert in the relationship can serve the introverted spouse by venturing out into the world and finding community for them together as a couple. In sharing strengths, we balance each other out. We work better together than as individuals (Ecclesiastes 4:9-10).

We need to stop seeing our spouse's weaknesses as something we need to fix and instead shift to the idea that our individual strengths can be used to serve each other. The faster this light bulb fires off, the faster we move toward a thriving marriage.

Look for a moment at some of the main areas of contention between you and your spouse. There's a good chance that underneath the tension, you'll find a mismanaged use of strengths.

For example, some friends of ours who work together found a regularly occurring conflict every time they attempted to colead a staff meeting. (*Attempted* being the operative word.) She has the gift of words; he has the gift of discernment. Each sufficiently lacks the other's gift. She loves to use her gift with words to wisely instruct, offer kind encouragement, and tell meaningful stories. He likes to get right to the point. What she struggles with, from time to time, is discerning when it's time to stop sharing and let someone else have a turn to talk as well.

What her gift lacks, however, her husband possesses in abundance. He has the unique ability to observe and sense what's happening in others—in this scenario, when their staff members' eyes have glazed over and they've stopped listening.

If this couple could leverage each other's strengths, acknowledging and valuing each other's gift, they could be an incredible team. He could lean on her gift with words to help accurately express what needs to be clearly communicated to their staff, and she could lean on his discernment to know when it's time to stop talking and allow others to share.

Notice that accessing this dynamic starts with acknowledging and affirming our spouse's gifts, rather than railing on their weaknesses. For example, if this husband says, "Would you stop talking already?" to his wife in the middle of their staff meeting, how do you think she'll respond? Not well, probably. If instead, before the meeting, he took the time to go over what needed to be shared and asked her to use her wonderful gift of words to communicate it, the meeting would be way more effective, and they would grow in their relationship and their ability to function well together as a team.

This is what it looks like to lend our strengths to one another.

THE CYCLE OF SERVING
JENNI ————————————————————————

A continual pattern we have experienced in our own marriage is something we like to call the cycle of serving. Essentially, the more we cultivate this consistent rhythm of serving one other, step-by-step, it's like a cycle we find ourselves in, moving us toward each other and toward closeness. It doesn't happen all at once, but over time, each choice to serve one another adds up and eventually we look up to find ourselves in a beautiful place of deep connection and strength, wondering how we ever got so blessed to have each other and feeling so grateful for our marriage.

The opposite is true as well. The more we make small choices to neglect each other's needs, the more we find ourselves in a downward cycle, step-by-step, choice by choice, moving further and further away from each other and from the life we want. Eventually we look up and start to wonder how in the world we got here and why we feel so distant from each other. Somewhere along the way, our focus shifted from *How can I meet their needs?* to *I wish they would just wake up and meet my needs!*

If you find yourself in this place today, I want to pause and encourage you. The good news is, friend, we are always one step away from reversing the cycle and moving back in the right direction by choosing to serve. We are always one choice away from moving toward the life and marriage we long for.

Now, I know from experience that when we're at the bottom of this cycle, completely out of rhythm, going out of our way to serve someone who seems like they're not even trying to meet our needs can feel like the very last thing on earth we want to do. But it's right here in this place of feeling they don't deserve it where the greatest possibility for change can occur. We have the power to start a cycle of change. We can be the one to reach out and start to meet those needs. We can be the catalyst for healing.

I promise you—as you choose to enter their world, see them

We have the power to start a cycle of change.

for who they truly are, listen well, and lend your strengths, you will watch your relationship start to move toward the place you both long for. It's almost impossible to stick your feet in the ground and continue to maintain a behavior that is mean and selfish when someone is going out of their way to lovingly care for you and meet your needs. Give it a try.

Remember, friends—change takes time. True growth is always slow growth. But the more you practice this rhythm of serving, the more you will see a difference in your marriage, and the closer you will move toward the life you both long to live. Love never fails (1 Corinthians 13:8). Keep going.

PRACTICE

- Take some time to listen to your spouse's life this week. Ask them to share ways you could serve that would be particularly meaningful to them.

- Create a daily habit of serving your spouse. Find a small, specific daily task that you can do to communicate love to your spouse and consistently practice it.

- What is something your spouse has asked you to do for a while now? Change the light bulbs in the hallway? Hang the curtains? Plan a date night? Initiate intimacy? Reflect over your conversations and choose just one thing you could surprise them with this week.

- Where is your spouse uniquely gifted? Take a moment this week to look, notice, and name just one area where your spouse shines.

6

STEP INTO
THE PAINTING

The Rhythm of Slowing Down

Teach us to number our days,
that we may gain a heart of wisdom.

PSALM 90:12

Spend the afternoon. You can't take it with you.

ANNIE DILLARD

JENNI

At the end of every episode of our podcast, *Live It Well*, we always close with the same question: "What advice would you give to the younger you?" It's easily my very favorite part of the show. Given no time to prepare, each guest just instinctively pulls out the very first thing that comes to mind. One answer I've never been able to shake came from Mark and Jan Foreman, the authors of our favorite parenting book, *Never Say No*. They simply replied, "Step into the painting."[1]

What does it mean to step into the painting? When you drive by a glowing sunset, don't just keep driving; pull over and take it in. When your kids are playing in the park, don't just sit and watch them; get off the park bench and join them. When everyone starts to feel the beat and jumps up to let it loose on the living-room floor, don't you dare be caught sitting on the sidelines; dance like no one's watching. The very best parts of our day, our week, and our life will be the moments we choose to slow down and savor. Stepping into the painting is the practice that can transform passing moments into precious memories.

Stepping into the painting is the practice that can transform passing moments into precious memories.

I was reminded of this rhythm the very next night after our interview with the Foremans. I *may* have been in the girls' closet, painstakingly organizing their freshly cleaned laundry according to the classic Roy G. Biv order (don't judge) when I heard voices coming from inside their little pink tepee. The sweetest story time was taking place between Chris and the girls. And I heard the invitation: *Step into the painting.*

I'll be honest, the Enneagram One in me wanted to just stay in the closet and finish organizing the clothes. After all, I had only made it to green, and I still had blue, indigo, and violet to finish, for crying out loud! Thankfully, the prompting continued as I remembered something else Jan had mentioned during our time together: The most meaningful part of your day will never be working on the laundry.[2]

That was all I needed. I put down the laundry, ran around

the corner, and leaped into the pink tepee, hoping I wasn't too late. The girls both squealed in excitement to see Mommy jumping in to join them, and we all finished the bedtime story together, wrapped up in each other's arms, closing out with a hearty singalong of "Jesus Loves Me." Our oldest daughter heard us from down the hall as we started singing, and she ran into the tepee to join, as well. Suddenly, we found ourselves in the middle of a golden moment, all snuggled up together in that tepee, singing at the top of our lungs. Chris and I glanced at each other, with a look that said, *Yep. This is where it's at. Right here. Life just doesn't get any better than this.* These are the moments that make up the life we long for. *Life that is truly life.* And I almost missed it, for laundry.

Busyness. It might just be the most dangerous sin of all because it doesn't really feel like one. But busyness, hurry, and distraction have the greatest potential to steal the most joy from our lives. And joy, as a friend recently reminded me, is actually where our strength comes from (Nehemiah 8:10). When we say yes to the people in our lives who matter most, when we choose to be completely present, hearts fully alive and filled with gratitude for this gift of life, delighting in God and in our people, we are at our strongest. It's almost as if joy builds a shield of protection all around us, guarding us against the destructive distractions and busyness of the world. We will never truly enjoy our lives, our relationships, and our moments if we're just rushing from one activity to the next.

> Love simply cannot grow when we're in too much of a hurry to cultivate it.

Love simply cannot grow when we're in too much of a hurry to cultivate it. Love only grows when we slow down long enough to cherish the people right in front of us, open our eyes to see the beauty they carry, and simply receive the delight of being fully present with them. True connection—giving our full, undistracted attention—is one of the best gifts we can give to our spouse, our kids, and to all the relationships we value most.

As Ronald Rolheiser says, "We know that life is passing us by and we are so preoccupied with the business of making a living and the duties of family and community that only rarely is there any time to actually live. It seems that there is never any unpressured time, unhurried time, undesignated time, leisure time, time to smell the flowers, time to simply luxuriate in being alive."[3]

Thriving couples say yes to the small moments together.

Don't hear what I'm not saying. I'm not for a minute suggesting we blow off our responsibilities as adults to spend the day in bed with our spouse or playing make-believe with our kids. Slowing won't make the chores disappear, but it will keep them from zapping our energy and joy for life and for those around us. Thriving couples say yes to the small moments together.

Rolheiser, noting David Steindl-Rast, says, "Leisure is not the privilege of those who have time, but rather the virtue of those who give to each instant of life the time it deserves."[4] Yes, there are countless things that need to be done over the course of a day. But the way in which we accomplish them does not have to mean plowing over or completely ignoring those we love, therefore stripping all meaning and connection from our day. There is magic in the meantime.

SLOWING FOR CONNECTION

Teach us to number our days,
that we may gain a heart of wisdom.

PSALM 90:12

I love that Proverbs says, "*Teach* us to number our days." We
need to be *taught*. As we've learned already on this journey
together, the first step toward change is always honesty . . . fol-
lowed shortly by (gulp) repentance. Saying no to the lies of this
world and yes to the truth of God. So we begin by crying out
to the Lord to pour His wisdom into our hearts. *Teach* us, Lord,
to make our days *count*. To open our eyes to see what truly matters most and to communicate our love by slowing down long
enough to build true connection.

Numbering our days means remembering that they are a
gift from God—and that before we know it, they will all be
gone. When we live from this mindset, we can walk through
life with great intention, slowing down and saying yes to what
truly matters most.

We also may need to take a moment to sit across from our
spouse, look them in the eye, and say, "I'm sorry. I haven't given
you my whole heart and my full presence." It's amazing how a
simple apology can wipe the slate clean and give you a fresh
start. It's far too easy to get sidetracked from the vision we
have for our marriage. As we get so busy with countless other
"important" things in life, we can start to feel disconnected.

When was the last time you felt truly connected to your
spouse? Have we spent more time lately asking them for support with the kids or assistance with the chores than we have
about their life and their dreams and the state of their soul? The

pace of life can rob from us the ability to cultivate rich love, joy, and meaning in our closest relationships. Which is actually the point. But here's the good news: There are countless invitations for us to choose to slow down and turn our attention back toward each other, to step into the painting.

In his extensive research on why some couples last while others crumble, research psychologist Dr. John Gottman describes these invitations for emotional connection as "bids" from our spouse that we can choose to either turn away from or turn toward in our response. Gottman Institute blogger Ellie Lisitsa explains:

> Every time you turn towards your partner's bids for emotional connection, you are making a deposit in . . . your Emotional Bank Account. You add value to your account when you create and build on positive moments between yourself and your partner. These little moments add up, reminding the two of you of the feelings you have for one another and of your commitment to supporting each other.[5]

After studying thousands of newlywed couples, Dr. Gottman found that the couples who chose to answer their spouse's "bid" for connection 86 percent of the time while being observed were found to be happily married six years later, while the couples who only turned toward their spouse 33 percent of the time during the study were divorced within six years.[6]

Each little moment of slowing down and saying yes to our spouse matters. Over time, we build an incredible foundation for our life together. When difficult times come, as they always do—from navigating everyday conflicts to weathering the most tragic of calamities—we either have a strong account of emotional connection to draw from or not. Couples who can weather the storms of life and resolve conflicts well do so not because they are masters at conflict resolution but because they are able to draw from and lean on a strong emotional connection with their spouse. In other words, they have a relationship worth fighting for.

> Each little moment of slowing down and saying yes to our spouse matters.

Sometimes, what we need most is simply to step in and be fully present to the moment right in front of us. To slow dance with our spouse in the kitchen. To lean in and listen as they pour out their heart to us. To pour a glass of wine, light a candle, and curl up together on the back porch. To laugh until our sides ache. As Eugene Peterson said, "Some insights are only accessible while laughing."[7]

No matter where this finds us in our emotional connection to our spouse, strong or weak, the great news is, we can begin today. We can choose to say yes to our spouse's invitations for connection. These opportunities can be anything from "Hey, did you read that article?" to "Hey, do you want to make love?" Simply the act of engaging them, of stopping whatever we're doing to show interest in our spouse and what they are saying to us, builds the connection that will add up over time. Every time we slow down to truly connect with our spouse leads us—step-by-step—closer to a thriving marriage.

Intentional Slowing

Take the following hurry inventory:

HURRY INVENTORY

What moments during your week do you find yourself most in a hurry?

....

....

....

....

What happens as you relate to your spouse in those moments?

....

....

....

....

What are some ways you can intentionally eliminate hurry around those activities?

....

....

....

....

When I did this inventory, I found that, like a lot of families, Chris and I were the most hurried in the morning: getting the kids up and fed, finding shoes and homework, making lunches, and finally rushing out the door. This frantic tornado is not my favorite way to start the day. For some reason, hurry at this time of day seemed to bring out the very worst in all of us. So, as Dallas Willard famously said, "to ruthlessly eliminate hurry,"[8] we began preparing everything the night before: assemble lunches, lay out / agree on outfits (did we mention we have a lot of girls?), make sure all textbooks and homework papers are packed and ready to go. It's amazing how a little preparation can transform the morning from utter chaos to peaceful and even enjoyable.

In the afternoons, we found that when Chris would walk in the door from work still on his phone, somehow it threw off the rest of the evening. But instead, when he intentionally wraps up any calls or lingering work on his phone before he walks in the door, he communicates to me and to the kids that he is all ours, which sets an important tone for connection for the rest of the night.

What are some areas in your life where you feel most hurried? Ask your spouse if there are times they feel you are most distracted or rushed. What are some intentional ways you can proactively say yes to your spouse in those moments? This requires paying attention. Maybe your spouse has already been asking for a date night for months. Maybe they've dropped a hint or two about going camping together. Maybe they're exploring what's next in their career and need your full attention to help talk them through it. Maybe it's been a while since you've been the one to initiate intimacy. Our job is to take notice, make a plan, and slow down to meet them there.

What are some ways you can support your spouse and their need to slow down? When do they typically need more care or rest? Try to notice the recurring needs your spouse has and support them in filling them. Is there a time during the week you've noticed your spouse reaches the end of their tank? Think of ways you could help remove some burdens, so they have the margin to slow down and fill it back up.

It's also important to pay attention to your own breaking points and let your spouse know what the warning signs look like. Intentionally slowing down, on a regular basis, to care for yourself means taking time to replenish your own soul so that you can love your people well without burning out.

Of course, each person is unique in the ways their tank is filled. For me, in this current season with five wild, wonderful kids in our home, I need quiet. I need solitude. I need trees. Chris supports my thriving by watching the kids so I can go for a run in the trails or enjoy an unhurried quiet time at my favorite coffee shop. My mom, however, is the opposite. She is an extreme extrovert in a season of life with no kids in the house, living deep in the country, with no one around. So, to support her flourishing, my dad has encouraged her to join women's Bible studies, suggested she spend the afternoon with a new friend, and even sent her off for a week away with girlfriends.

Find what makes your spouse come alive and support them in making it happen.

Find what makes your spouse come alive and support them in making it happen. If both of you are living out of fullness and restoration, your marriage will thrive.

In each moment when we are tempted to hurry through to the next thing or keep pushing through when we know we're spent, we can choose to slow down instead. We can intentionally prepare in advance so that we can create space to enjoy our spouse, unhurried and fully present.

Spontaneous Slowing

Slowing down can't always be scheduled. We must develop the habit of choosing to say yes to the people in front of us, even if it feels inconvenient or uncomfortable. This might mean putting down the phone and look-ing your spouse in the eye. Or turning off the TV to really listen to what they're trying to say. Or it may mean leaving the laundry for later to join in the family story time. Now, I under-stand, this isn't always possible. There are things we simply must get done—but that's less often the case than we tend to believe. The point is this: Don't let *anything* steal the gift of know-ing and loving your people well. This day, this moment, is a great gift. Often the joy we lack is hiding in the invitations all around us to slow down and enjoy the moment.

> Often the joy we lack is hiding in the invitations all around us to slow down and enjoy the moment.

Time equals love. We cannot simultaneously view life as a gift and rush right through it. Savoring it, cherishing it, requires slowing.

WHO WE BECOME

CHRIS ——————————————————————————

Often the lessons God is trying to teach me come through rep-etition at every turn. A book I'm reading, a Scripture in my morning quiet time, a sermon, a conversation with a friend—a theme will start to emerge. Lately this is it: What is my soul becoming? What matters most, more than all the good things we are involved in, activities we enjoy, dreams we are chasing, is the soul we are becoming.

This wonderful gift of life is over before we know it, and

what matters most, much to our surprise, is not our list of achievements, trophies, and awards. It's not even all the good deeds we can accomplish or the responsible tasks we complete. It's who we become. The truth is, if we drink the Kool-Aid being sold to us by pushing aside everything and everyone in the way of achieving our dreams, we may, in fact, achieve those dreams, but we will also leave a wake of destruction behind us, both in our relationships and in our own souls.

This is the reason some of the most "successful" people in the world reach the end of the wrong rainbow and implode. Because ambition kills. If the dreams we are pursuing do not form us into the person God has called us to become, they have the potential to destroy us, robbing us of everything we hold dear. The dreams God calls us to pursue, the ones that build His Kingdom, will never dismiss or destroy others in our path or cause us to forfeit our souls. They will always bring joy, life, and peace to us as well as those around us, and they will form us into the person He created us to become. What matters is the wake we leave behind. What matters is who we become.

> What matters is the wake we leave behind. What matters is who we become.

If I come to the end of my life and I have never written a *New York Times* bestseller, built a million-dollar company, or achieved any success in the world's eyes but I have become a gentle, loving, generous, grateful, kind human being, I will receive the only recognition that really matters: "Well done, good and faithful servant" (Matthew 25:23).

May we be people who remember what matters most.

So let's take the vow of slowing down together. Let's take hold of the everyday moments of joy right in front of us. Say no to distractions, no to hurry, and a big yes to the people and experiences right in front of us. Step-by-step, we choose to build the strong connection that leads to the thriving marriage we long for. May you and I become unhurried people. Fully alive, fully present, fully cherishing those we love most.

PRACTICE

- Where are the areas you feel most hurried?

- Throughout your week, keep a running list of times where hurry is creeping in. What are some ways you can proactively eliminate hurry from those areas of your life?

- Be on the lookout for opportunities to slow down and step into the painting this week.

- Make a mental note of your yeses and nos this week. Who and what are you giving your yeses to? How can you shift your schedule and priorities to allow for more yeses to go to those you love most?

- Put a date on the calendar to soak up a sunset together this week.

7

STAY AWAKE

AND ALIVE

The Rhythm of Seeking Adventure

If you never leave home, never let go,
you'll never make it to the great unknown.

BEAR AND BO RINEHART

Wake up from your sleep ... Christ will show you the light!

EPHESIANS 5:14, MSG

CHRIS

Our friend Erin began to notice that something just wasn't quite right with her husband, Noah. He was meeting every metric of the typical American dream. He had a steady job where he was moving up in the ranks and increasing his paycheck every year. Their family was comfortable. They had a lovely house, a sizable savings account, and plenty of safety and security. But over time, Erin began to sense a restlessness in Noah, a desire for something more, a longing for a new adventure. They both began to wonder if the Lord might be calling them to more than just the comfortable life they were living.

As Dr. Henry Cloud writes, "One of the worst things you can die with is potential. Die with failures before you die with potential. Potential is something to be realized, not guarded and protected."[1] This was the thought keeping our friends Noah and Erin awake at night. They knew they had more to give, and to reach the potential inside them, they needed to take an appropriate risk.

"We just couldn't shake the sense that God's best was waiting for us on the other side of our being willing to move past our comfort zone," Erin told us.

"Deep down, I knew we were missing out on the great by holding on to the good," Noah shared. "Something in me just felt like it wasn't being used and was actually starting to die."[2]

A bit of a self-proclaimed "tech nerd," Noah began to dream of starting an app-development business on the side, and he made the rookie mistake of mentioning this idea to me. And here's what you need to know—over time, people in my life have nicknamed me the "Fire Starter." Because if you share even the "spark" of a dream around me, I'm going to pour gas on that joker and set a forest fire in your heart, so you have no choice but to follow that dream and bring it to life. Not long after our conversation, Noah took the calculated leap to see his dream become a reality. Years later, this huge first step eventually landed him as a cofounder and CTO of a startup valued in millions of dollars. He bought me a fire-starter kit as a thank-you.

Over the years, I've been honored to be a part of seeing many adventures and dreams come to life. I've had the pleasure to see a friend start a food truck that, for years, he had only scribbled on paper. One friend wrestled for five years before he finally took the leap from his day job to start the creative agency he'd envisioned in his heart for so long. And just yesterday, I received a text from a couple who are living out the adventure of their life together.

I met Megan and Mitchel around 2015 while pastoring a local church in Keller, Texas. I found myself in Megan's stylist chair at Sport Clips. While she cut my hair, the typical small talk ensued, but with me being the kind of guy who can't live in small-talk land for very long, we quickly got to the good stuff: her dreams. She explained how she and her husband, Mitchel, lived in a tiny house with their two boys and that they had a dream to serve in youth ministry together someday. Now when I say tiny house, I mean an actual, on wheels, can-be-moved-down-the-road-a-few-miles "tiny house." Their desire for ministry was one they couldn't shake, but their lack of "experience" on paper was limiting their options of which jobs they qualified for.

I'm never one to let a piece of paper stand in the way of someone's dream. I offered to have lunch with Megan and Mitchel. It was a special hour at a local chicken joint where, over chicken and waffles, we crafted a strategy they could use to get their foot in the door of a church and begin the ministry journey they'd been dreaming of. But what I didn't know then was, the part of the conversation that spoke loudest to these two was when I shared about the adventures Jenni and I had taken over the years. The rhythm of adventure was just never something that had been modeled for them, and they had never even realized that they had permission to hitch that tiny house of theirs to the back of their truck and strike out on a wild adventure together. But that's just what they did.

Since that lunch years ago they have served in ministries all over the northwest and across the country. This is the message I got just yesterday from Megan and Mitchel: "Just reflecting today on our journey and wanted to say thank you. We are such risk-takers today and you are a *huge* part of that. We never would be where we are today had you never pushed us and modeled that lifestyle. So, thank you, biscuits and graebe."

UNDERSTANDING ADVENTURE

Why do we need adventure? And how in the world is adventure an essential part of a thriving marriage? The truth is, we're all wired for adventure. No one wants to get to the end of their life still holding on to a long list of things they wish they had done. We all want to look back with gratitude and marvel at all the incredible adventures we got to experience in our life together.

A life worth living needs a good dose of adventure.

If we are honest with ourselves, we all have specific dreams and desires for our life that are planted deep within us but that we choose to ignore for a number of reasons. Reasons that can be fully justified, yet not rationalized. But a life worth living needs a good dose of adventure.

When we stop adventuring, when we stop risking, we actually stop growing. When we allow fear or comfort or apathy to keep us from growing and changing and trying new things together, we run the risk of rusting out. As Jan Foreman puts it, "When you rustout, it's because you've made a habit of saying no to the opportunities that come along . . . There's too much of God in this universe to just sit and miss out on the opportunities He gives you."[3]

According to executive life coach Dr. Richard Leider and leadership coach Steven Buchholz,

> Rustout is the slow death that follows when we stop making choices that keep life alive. . . . Rustout means we are no longer growing, but at best, are simply maintaining. . . . Rustout is the opposite of burnout. Burnout is overdoing. Rustout is underbeing. Rustout occurs when our lives deteriorate through the disuse of our potential.[4]

Are we rusting out? Have we stopped growing? Have we given up on ourselves or on the hope that our life can look any different than it currently does? When was the last time you said yes to something new? When was the last time you said yes to a brave adventure together? Leider and Buchholz also note, "People who are experiencing rustout feel afraid to act. They're unwilling to do the very things that would make them feel alive. They end up sitting on the sidelines, while the dance of life goes on without them."[5]

Now, I realize there are some who want to skip this chapter altogether. Or think to themselves, *I'm good on the whole adventure thing*. And I totally get why you might feel that way. We are all wired differently. Honestly, if you're the "risk adverse" member of your dynamic duo, that's great—because more than likely you have been the voice of reason on a number of occasions. Jenni has been that voice of wisdom for me, and I'm so thankful for her. Adventure isn't about making wild moves, quitting your job, or moving across the country. The sense of adventure we've noticed in thriving couples across the board is more of a mindset of adventure; it's how you position your heart toward growth and change, toward your spouse and the life you're building together—how you honor the dreams and desires in your marriage by learning to say yes.

Dreams

Adventure is all about the heart. Living a life of adventure together must include staying in touch with the dreams and desires God has placed in our hearts. We can't have the vibrant, thriving marriage we desire if our hearts are no longer alive. Living the life we desire and having the kind of relationship we desire is going to require a heart that's fully awake and alive.

If we look up to find we've lost heart or rusted out somewhere along the way, step one is going back to ask ourselves: *What was it I once dreamed of? What was the last adventure God invited me into? What dream keeps rising to the top of my heart, and what is causing me to push it away?*

Maybe you've dreamed of moving to another city or adopting a child. Maybe you can't shake your desire to get your MBA or to stay home with your kids. A dream is anything worthwhile that keeps rising to the top of our heart. We all have dreams.

Part of loving each other well means reminding each other that God is not finished with us yet. There's never been a day like this one, and God is always up to something new (see Isaiah 43). I want eyes to see it! I don't want to sleepwalk through life. I want to be awake and alive, eyes wide open to the new thing that God is doing right in front of me. I want to lean in and be a vital part of it. And because my spouse is now a part of me, I am no longer only aware of my own well-being. I am committed to supporting the flourishing of my spouse as well. This means we get to remind each other what brings us life and makes us come alive.

> I've learnt that making a living is not the same thing as making a life.[6]
>
> MAYA ANGELOU

Practicing adventure is tapping into those wild, passionate dreams that you had when you first got married and taking the time to listen for new dreams and adventures God is calling you into along the way. It's remembering we are not here by accident and that God brought the two of us together with a specific purpose in mind. It's about navigating the blindsiding curveballs life throws at you and coming out on the other side stronger as a couple. Adventure pushes back on a life of apathy and comfort. A marriage and life leaned into adventure is one that is pleasing to the Lord.

It can be as simple as the spontaneous choice to dance with your spouse on a Saturday morning while making pancakes, or surprising them with flowers or a date night. Adventure is supporting your wife when she shares the dream of going back to school to get her MBA. Adventure is living your life with the knowledge that as Christ followers and as a couple, your life and marriage are not your own. On the day we stood before God and said "I do," we were committing to share our life, not a mere existence of comfort and safety but the greatest adventure of our lives!

Desires

Adventure is prevention against apathy, the feeling of *not* feeling. Sometimes the message we receive as followers of Christ is that spiritual growth means killing our dreams and desires. But that's not actually the life that's offered to us at all. As author John Eldredge says, "Christianity begins with an invitation to desire."[7]

Just as a growing hunger for God is the key to life, a deepening desire for our spouse is also key to a thriving marriage. We must keep our fire for God and for each other alive and growing. We may not always have the same kind of electric spark we had at the very beginning of the relationship, but we *can* have a roaring flame that grows deeper and stronger with time.

Imagine diving into the ocean. There's nothing like that feeling when your skin first hits the water. But once you're in, you're in. You're immersed. The journey has begun. There's no going back and re-creating that first feeling of hitting the water, and spending our efforts trying to recover it will only leave us frustrated and exhausted. *But* the good news is, there are endless mysteries, adventures, and discoveries that lie ahead as we venture out into the deeper water.

Love is that way. With each day, we're meant to move beyond the shallows in our marriage and further and further out into the beauty and delight of swimming in deep water. We weren't meant to shrink back from what God is calling us to. We're meant for lives of courage, lives awake and alive to where the Spirit leads us. He's not finished yet. There is always something more God has for us, more to see, more to do, more to become—together.

Apathy is dangerous for a marriage. If we ignore our longing for more, our longing for newness and discovery, our need to feel the fresh wind of change in our face, this restlessness can start to surface in other ways. John Eldredge warns against the danger we face when we "bury [our] heart under the porch and seek a safer life."[8]

Complacency is a deadly foe of all spiritual growth.[9]

A. W. TOZER

When we catch ourselves longing for something we don't yet have, let's not immediately shame, rebuke, and dismiss the feeling. A better response might be to ask ourselves, *What healthy desire could this be pointing to?* and *What would it look like for me to put my time, attention, and energy into making this dream a reality in my own life?*

If you see a couple, for example, whose love and admiration for each other stops you in your tracks, don't just immediately label the longing you have as jealousy and scold yourself. What if instead you acknowledged the longing, asked God what good desire this could be pointing to, then looked for ways to cultivate that kind of love and admiration in your own relationship? What obstacles are standing in the way? How can you proactively work to remove them?

Yes, we will all go through seasons of sameness, and not everything predictable and routine can lead to rusting out. But when we allow fear to keep us from making new, healthy changes, we enter the danger zone. Adventure stirs desire. And desire, when surrendered to God, is a gift that can bring us to the life He has for us.

Saying Yes

JENNI ──────────────────────────────────

At the beginning of each new year, Chris and I both choose a word, a theme to guide the 365 days ahead. I love the whole process—quieting myself to hear from the Lord, leaning in to sense what He's stirring in my heart and life for the coming year. Without fail, each year I always start off thinking I know the exact reason for the word and what it means for the future. Then, each time, the Lord begins to peel it back, layer by layer, to reveal new meanings, new significance for the word and the reasons I need it.

One year my word was *dance*. Just hang with me; it's not what it sounds like. No, I didn't have hidden dreams to become a professional dancer or anything like that. As soon as it came to me, I was simultaneously excited and embarrassed. Like opening a Christmas gift to find a bright pair of neon pants that you sort of like but also don't really want to wear in public. I pictured our friends rolling their eyes as we all went around the room to share our words for the year. But, nevertheless, God's quiet voice was undeniable. *Dance*. And I knew why.

A few weeks prior, my daughter and I had been dancing in the kitchen together, most likely to some glorious 1980s pop music. (Sidenote: Just try to stay in a grumpy mood while blasting "Uptown Girl" . . . It's pretty much impossible.) She was wrapped up in my arms, her legs wound securely around my waist as we danced. I leaned forward for the climactic dip and spin, and I watched as she just let her arms fly all the way out as I spun her around and around on the smooth wood floor. I'll never forget the look on her face. Pure bliss. It very easily could have been one of absolute terror, for in reality, if I had let her go, she would have gone flying clear across the room. But it wasn't. All she felt was sheer joy because she trusted me completely.

I couldn't stop thinking about that joy on her face. How I longed to live like that. To trust God the way she trusted me. To find the strength to let go with complete confidence, knowing that He had me. That no matter what happened, He would never let me go. I realized I'd been clinging for dear life to safety, for fear that He'd drop me. What joy, what exhilaration had I been forfeiting all because I refused to trust?

I needed to change. I wanted to trust, and for maybe the first time in my life, I was more afraid of staying than going. More afraid of rusting out than of following Jesus out into the great unknown. More afraid of what would happen if I remained, safe on the sidelines, than if I took the risk to join in the dance. I wanted to live from a place of trust, like my daughter. I wanted to let go and dance.

I have come that they may have life,
and have it to the full.
JOHN 10:10

Some of us are more reluctant to say yes to adventure than others. Chris does not have a fearful bone in his body. In fact, he seems to thrive in situations that make most people break out in hives. He's at his absolute best under pressure and is always down for a fresh adventure. For the first five years of our marriage, I was in for all of it. We were both so eager to experience as much life as we possibly could, we moved to a different city every single year. New jobs, new houses, new people and places. Part of it was exhilarating, and part of it, after a while, became exhausting. After we had our second child, I started to ache for stability. And family. We both sensed it was time to finally drop our anchor and start to put down roots.

So we did. Through His grace, God provided a wonderful job for Chris as a local church pastor, and we were able to live in the Dallas–Fort Worth area for a solid, blissful decade. Roots.

Depth. Community. It was *beautiful*. Exactly what the Lord knew we needed. The relationships and experiences during that sweet season of our lives marked us forever and laid the strongest foundation for us as a growing family. Mentors shaped us. Lifelong relationships were born. Friends became family. A city finally became a home.

And then. Toward the end of that delightful decade of growing roots, of sweet sameness and consistency, the winds of change gently began to blow again. I resisted at first. And by resisted, I mean, rebuked. Renounced. Rejected.

But the whispers of adventure just kept gently coming. Everywhere I went, every sermon, every book, every podcast, conversation, and even my children's cartoons all began to whisper the same steady message. He was clearly inviting us into something new. He does not force us, of course. The choice is always ours. But a new adventure was awaiting—that much we knew for certain. The question became, would we choose to join Him or not? Would we cling to comfort or choose to follow Him out on the water again?

> For everything there is a season,
>   a time for every activity under heaven. . . .
> A time to cry and a time to laugh.
>   A time to grieve and a time to dance. . . .
>   A time to embrace and a time to turn away.
>
> ECCLESIASTES 3:1, 4-5, NLT

At the end of that year, the year I felt God calling me into trust, Chris and I found ourselves sitting in that very same corner of the living room where God had given the word *dance* to guide the year. This time, we were surrounded by our dearest Texas friends, who had become like family to us, as they lovingly prayed and cried and launched us into a brand-new season. A new beginning for our not-so-little-anymore family of seven, states away from the place that felt most like home.

Maybe you've been feeling God stirring something in you for a while now, an invitation into a brave, new adventure. What is it that keeps you from saying yes? As pastor Tyler Staton says, "Your comfort zone robs you of way more than it gives you."[10] Practicing adventure does not have to be something as drastic as moving across the country or as life-changing as an adoption. It can be anything the Lord is stirring in your heart: volunteering at the local homeless shelter, mentoring a younger couple, or committing to write that book. Or it could be as simple as praying the prayer that informs the Lord that you are ready for whatever adventure He has planned for you. Every person and every couple has a unique call and adventure that the Lord has purposed for their life together.

> Thriving couples stay awake and alive by saying yes to new adventures God invites them into.

There's not a human alive who won't benefit from a regular dose of adventure. I love what behavioral scientist Jon Levy says: "The true gift of adventure is not in achieving some goal, but in the person you become in the process."[11] Of course, the definition of adventure is different for everyone. What feels like adventure to me may not at all to you. The point is that *we all need it*. For a thriving marriage, we must keep saying yes to new adventures to keep each other from growing stagnant. As Levy notes, "The size of your life is in direct proportion to how uncomfortable you are willing to be."[12]

We must refuse to become fearful, shrinking back from the life God has called us to. Thriving couples stay awake and alive by saying yes to new adventures God invites them into. He is always up to something new, and there will always be new places with God we're invited to go.

I love what Irish poet John O'Donohue writes:

There should always be a healthy tension between the life we have settled for and the desires that still call us. In this sense our desires are the messengers of our unlived life, calling us to attention and action while we still have time here to explore fields where the treasure dwells![13]

Adventure can look as small as trying out something new together. Call a sitter and surprise him with a romantic night at a new hotel, or invite that new couple over for dinner. Whether it's stepping out to start a new small group or trusting God to starting a new company, you develop the rhythm of adventure together by refusing to stay comfortable, following God's lead as a couple, and trusting Him for the outcome.

So, let's step into adventure and let Deuteronomy 31:7 be our compass: "Be strong and courageous, for you must go." Adventure is calling, and the first step starts with . . . *yes!*

RECKLESS OR ADVENTUROUS

Before we continue, I think it's important to point out the difference between a healthy sense of adventure and just a harmful recklessness. Healthy adventure is calculated, considering wisdom and guidance. It's willing to risk, but only as the Lord leads and for the greater purpose of growth and change. Recklessness is brash and careless, risking for the thrill of it alone, and doesn't pause to consider wisdom before taking the leap. This is far from the healthy rhythm of adventure we're talking about. The adventures God invites us into will never lead us to be reckless with those we love, including our spouse.

> Healthy adventure is calculated, considering wisdom and guidance.

As we mentioned earlier, opposites tend to attract. Usually in a marriage, one person leans more naturally toward adventure, and the other likes their feet planted firmly on the ground. We must recognize the strengths both bring to the relationship as we set out to cultivate rhythms of adventure in our life together. Without the safe person, the adventurer can easily fall into recklessness, pursuing the next big thrill just for the high of it. Listen to your spouse to see where they're comfortable risking and where they're not.

So what does this rhythm look like for us? How do we cultivate a heart that's fully awake and alive? How do we intentionally begin to practice this rhythm of adventure? We've noticed three ways healthy couples consistently bring this rhythm to life: water each other's dreams, give each other room to grow and change, and offer each other freedom to fly.

Water Each Other's Dreams

Keep alive the dream; for as long as a man has a dream in his heart, he cannot lose the significance of living.

HOWARD THURMAN

When Steve first met his future wife, Sarah, he quickly discovered she had a dream to start a women's magazine. Not just any women's magazine, but the first women's magazine committed to bring dignity back to the feminine identity by implementing a "no retouching policy." Sarah had a lot of beautiful vision and passion, but what she needed was someone to help turn her dream into a reality. She needed Steve. Steve chose to get behind Sarah's dream by helping her set up a website and get a Kickstarter campaign started, and she was off to the races. Before long Sarah's magazine was featured in Anthropologie stores, Whole Foods, and independent boutiques nationwide.

The benefit Steve didn't see coming was as he poured himself out to help Sarah bring her dream to life, a dream also sparked within his own heart: to start a successful adventure company that created transformative experiences to develop a healthy identity in men.

"One of those things that has been the most personally impactful," Steve says, "has been coming alongside Sarah and like helping get her dream off the ground. . . . It's just so good to take your eyes off your own dream and like pour as much energy as you can into someone else's, even if it's just for a season."[14]

Do you know your spouse's dreams? What are their greatest passions? When was the last time you asked? Take the time this week to listen to your spouse's dreams or to help them uncover them for the first time. Look for clues. It could be something as simple as a passing comment or the way their eyes light up doing something they love. Great adventures are born when we begin to look for those small insights into one another and choose to take them seriously.

We each enter marriage as a whole person, carrying dreams, talents, and desires of our own. Having a thriving marriage means caring about and taking seriously the dreams for our life together that we both carry. Remember, it is impossible to love someone well without entering into their world. The healthiest couples take the time to find out their spouse's dreams and then partner with them to bring those dreams to life.

No one's opinion and support mean more to them than yours. No one. We have been given the unbelievable honor and sobering responsibility of being the most powerful person in our spouse's life. Their dreams are tender things. We must be careful and wise as we wade alongside them into the delicate waters of their deepest dreams and desires.

Thriving couples believe that there is room enough in their life for both people—for both sets of dreams. The truth is, if you ignore your spouse's dreams and desires long enough, they will eventually stop trying to tell you, and either their dreams will die or they will find someone else who will listen to and value them. Seeing your marriage as an opportunity for adventure means listening for the dreams God may be calling you to pursue together.

Once you know your spouse's dreams, you can become a part of bringing those dreams to life. What are some ways you can begin to water their dreams and watch them grow? Does she love to paint? Do you want to travel more together? Start a garden? Go on more dates just the two of you? What can you do to make these things a reality? You'll be amazed at the love that can grow in your relationship simply by showing your spouse that you're willing to support their dreams.

Permission to Change

Another key part of what allows us to practice the rhythm of adventure is giving each other permission to change. What does that mean, exactly? We can be married to many different versions of the same spouse throughout our life together. Neither of us is meant to remain stagnant. We're constantly changing and growing, moving and shifting, hopefully becoming more and more who we truly are, someone who looks more and more like Jesus. It's one of the greatest gifts of marriage! We get a front-row seat to the wild adventure of our spouse's life. What a gift we can be to each other when we choose to freely offer the support, encouragement, and room to watch each other fly.

As Wes Yoder says, "The early years of marriage are a time of vibrant self-discovery . . . If you keep your heart and your love alive, the transformation you will experience is no less remarkable than the day you took your first step or spoke your first word. The words and steps you take together are like a great awakening, a journey begun, a new language of the soul."[15]

When I first met Jenni as a young twentysomething in the early 2000s, she was singing in a Christian pop band (think NSYNC and Britney Spears), wearing pleather pants and a headset mic, dancing on stage to Christian pop songs, and occasionally rapping. Not kidding. But before long, she traded her pleather pants in for her beloved blue jeans, discovered a stack of spiritual-formation books, and was never the same. Today, I am happy to report, she's way more of the tree-loving,

granola-making, James Taylor–listening, Henri Nouwen–
reading Jesus hippy that we all know and love. When I see her
now, I'm seeing someone who's way more settled in herself than
the young Jenni I first met. But it takes a long time, and many
years of trial and error, to discover who we truly are. We must
give each other grace, permission, and support along the way,
as we try on new things to see what fits.

Throughout our marriage I have been an MTV reality-TV
personality, a traveling speaker, a pastor, a professional yo-yoer
(true story), and an entrepreneur, just to name a few. These
days, at forty, Jenni and I are both much more comfortable
in our own skin, with a much clearer idea of who we are and
what God's called us to do with our lives. But it has been quite
a winding path with many twists and turns to get us here. The
key components that helped us weather the ever-changing landscape of our desires, hobbies, dreams, bodies (dad bods are in,
right?), and vision for our marriage was keeping Christ at the
center and giving each other permission to try new things to
see what fits.

Thriving couples give each other permission to change and
grow, always committing to fiercely loving one another along
the way.

Freedom to Fly

Adventure needs space and opportunity. Remember, you both
entered this marriage with dreams and abilities of your own.
It's not enough to just acknowledge that those dreams exist.
Thriving couples give each other the freedom to enjoy their life
and do what makes them come alive.

As we grow in life together, adding layer upon layer of

wonderful blessings, urgent demands, and important responsibilities, we can stop making time to even listen to the dreams
and desires God puts inside us. We can't allow that to happen.
We must give each other the freedom and support necessary
to go out and do what God's called us to. Not only does this
active advocacy for each other draw us closer together but it also
sparks desire within us toward our spouse by allowing us to see
them fully alive, in their element.

Of course, the opposite is true as well. When we become
insecure and controlling, needing our partner to be everything
for us or remain within the boundaries of our comfort zone,
we stop encouraging them to do the things they need to thrive.
Eventually, this behavior can build bitter resentment and even
begin to drive them away from us.

Just today, while I was working at my favorite coffee shop,
I overheard a woman a few tables away telling her friend how
amazing her husband was at golf. And she admitted that before
they got married, he was *really* good—like probably-could-
have-played-in-the-PGA good. But then she said something
that shook me to my core. She said that she issued an ultima-
tum to him when they got engaged years before. If he wanted
to marry her, he needed to let that dream of being a pro golfer
die and become an accountant instead.

As I heard this, something deep inside me shuddered, and
I couldn't help but think about this poor dude. What did he
do with that dream? With that gifting? Did part of him grow
resentful toward his wife? What happens now when he steps
onto a golf course? Does he wonder what might have been?

Fear is never a wise counselor. For this woman, it may have
been fear of the unknown or the uncertainty of not getting a

steady paycheck. And of course, I don't know him—maybe he couldn't wait to put that dream on the shelf and grab the ol' accountant pocket protector (no offense to my accountants out there). But my guess is, he will always carry a "what if" in his heart. And I'm reminded once again how thankful I am for a wife who values my dreams and gives me the freedom to fly.

Just a few months ago, I encountered an opportunity for a great adventure. While I was eating with some colleagues at one of the various restaurants scattered throughout the Bellagio hotel in Las Vegas, the invitation for adventure came knocking. The crew and I had just wrapped up two days of filming, and at dinner that night, I happened to sit beside a well-known businessman who has built many successful companies you would know. In between bites, he leaned over to me and commended me on a job well done over the past few days. He then asked if I wanted to host a video interview he had scheduled in Los Angeles for . . . tomorrow.

Now, if you have kids and travel at all for business, you know that the spouse holding down the fort at home is the real hero! Anytime I'm gone, Jenni is always very aware of my return date, when my plane lands, and at what time I will be walking through our front door. My gut reaction was to decline the offer because it had been three days already since I left, and I knew my superwoman back home was conserving just enough energy in the tank for one more day of flying solo.

Just before I respectfully declined, I asked him who it was he wanted me to interview. He set his fork down, wiped off his mouth with the corner of his napkin, and looked me right in the eyes: "Mike Tyson."

So I called Jenni. I told her about the wild adventure that lay

before me. But before I could even ask for her blessing, she said,
"Absolutely you're interviewing Mike Tyson! Go for it, babe.
We're cheering you on from home!" Man, I love that woman.

The next morning, my middle school dreams came true as
I jumped on my first ever private jet, headed to Tyson Ranch
headquarters, and had the incredible honor of interviewing Iron
Mike himself. As a bonus, right before the interview started,
five-time NBA World Champion Dennis Rodman walked
through the door and decided to jump in with us. I was a kid in
a candy store. It was one of those crazy, surreal experiences. An
adventure I will always remember.

Of course, this is a fun story to tell, but here's the key point:
When adventure came knocking, it wasn't my decision alone to
pursue it. Even though Jenni wasn't with me in Las Vegas, she is
on this wild ride called life with me, and her voice matters. She
could very easily have said, "Babe, come home. I'm exhausted,
and the kids miss you." I wouldn't have blamed her at all for
feeling that way, and I would have come straight home. But
together we saw a moment to say yes to an adventure, and we
took it. I went to LA physically alone, but I carried her with me
every step of the way.

Sometimes the situation is reversed, and I get to be the one
to cheer *her* on as she says yes to a dream. And the joy becomes
mine as well! You and I have been given the incredible opportunity to support the dreams and desires of our spouse. And
if we steward our impact well, we can take part in watching
them thrive. So, my question to you is, are you letting your
spouse fly? Are you saying yes when that inconvenient phone
call comes? As Stasi Eldredge says, "We long to be an irreplaceable part of a shared adventure."[16] Sometimes the adventure

involves both of us taking the leap together, and other times we get to play an irreplaceable role by supporting one another's adventures and making our voice the very loudest to cheer each other on.

THE MESSY MIDDLE

JENNI

"For some reason, I've been hitting a wall with this adventure chapter," I told our editor over the phone today as I nursed my last few drops of breakfast blend. She's all snuggled up in her book-lined den, sipping a steaming-hot latte as she looks out over the breathtaking mountain views of Colorado. At least that's how I picture her.

Chris and I know the power of this rhythm down to our bones. If you ask anyone close to us, they will tell you, this is one value that always rises to the top. This rhythm of adventure— we've experienced it our entire marriage, and we've seen it time and time again in thriving couples along the way. In many ways, our life together has felt like one big adventure after the next, and I know without a doubt just how crucial adventure is to a thriving marriage, but for some reason, communicating it right now is proving to be quite difficult.

Maybe it's the state of the world around us. This is definitely an interesting topic to be writing on in the middle of 2020. When we started this chapter, back in good ol' 2019, the world was a very, *very* different place. And then we entered 2020— the year of pandemic, of lockdowns, of saying no to things we thought we'd do and places we thought we'd go. This year has made me realize, among many other things, that it's very difficult to dream and seek adventure when the world around you is spinning. Mustering up the courage to say yes to new adventures, I realized, is a lot easier from a place of safety and security.

Maybe it's the fact that Chris and I are still smack-dab in the messy middle of our own gigantic adventure. Moving to a brand-new city after pastoring in the same town for almost ten years has been a harder adjustment than we ever dreamed it would be. We're no longer at the fun, exciting beginning part, still caught up in the rush of taking that first, breathtaking jump. And we're not quite to the other side either, where you stick your landing, strong and secure, taking in the beauty and blessing of a brand-new place. Able to look back at last and clearly see how much the journey was all worth it. No, we are still trudging along through the hard-but-necessary work in the messy middle of the journey, wondering when we'll make it to the other side. It's that part of the voyage where you have trouble remembering all the reasons that led you to jump in the first place.

So, hoping to get some fresh insights to pass along, I did what I often do when feeling stuck. I phoned a wise friend who has lived a *lot* more life than I have. He and his wife are not just any couple—he was my pastor growing up; his wife was my music teacher for six years, and they were the ones who actually married Chris and me seventeen years ago. So, needless to say, his words hold *weight*.

Talk to me about adventure, I said. What has it looked like in your life, over decades of marriage, the hard and the comfortable? The good and the bad? I asked him to tell me how it was all worth it, how it turned out for their good on the other side. (Actually, I don't think I asked that last question specifically, but I was so glad he must have read my mind because he answered it anyway.)

He told me their story of saying yes to a fresh adventure, of taking a big, brave jump to a brand-new city after pastoring in the same place for almost ten years. He told me how hard it was at first, how he wrestled with it for so long, but how ultimately, he knew he would be fighting the Lord's will to stay back. So, they jumped.

I couldn't believe it. He was literally describing our current situation almost exactly. I realized, as I listened, that this story was for me.

And then he said this:

> **There is no better place to be than in the path of obedience to the Lord.**
>
> Looking back now, all these years later, I can clearly see, there was a hole here, in this new place, a hole that was just the shape of our family that God was inviting us to fill. And so, we said yes. And trust me, it was hard at first—but we have zero regrets. Zero! It's been the greatest adventure of our lives.[17]

Tears immediately filled my eyes. I can't tell you how much I needed to hear those words. Maybe you needed to hear these words today too. Maybe right now you find yourself journeying through the messy middle of a daring adventure . . . not quite to the other side just yet. The thrill of the jump has worn off, and you find yourself right in the middle of the hardest part. Every great story has one. Maybe you need some encouragement to just keep going, to trust God to bring you safely and securely to the other side.

Friend, the adventures God calls us into are not promised to be easy; in fact, they rarely are. But we *are* promised that He will be *with us*, that He will never take us somewhere He Himself cannot be found, and that when we follow His lead, it will always be worth it on the other side. We will be *better* on the other side. The risk of following God's lead into the unknown is never as great as the risk of playing it safe when He's calling us out. Here's what I've learned:

There is no better place to be than in the path of obedience to the Lord.

Even when it's hard. Even when it looks nothing like you thought it would. There's no better place. He is *good*. His plans for us are so much better than the plans we dream up for ourselves. Saying yes to His adventures will always turn out to be for our good. It's always worth it.

It's worth it for the joy and the sheer life it brings to our soul. It's worth it for the hard work required to make it to the other side. It's worth it to be a vital part of the brand-new thing God is doing. I don't want to miss it. I don't want to rust out because I'm too afraid to say yes to the new thing. I don't want to give up when the adventure looks different than I thought it would.

Sometimes we misinterpret the mess in the middle to mean that God is no longer in it. That somehow if we reach a part of the story where things aren't going according to our plans, somehow God has exited stage right. But I love what author Katherine Wolf said to us in a recent interview: "So many people waste their lives chasing the way it used to be and not recognizing this is what God has put in front of me today, and

I'm going to live well into this, even though I never could have imagined this being my story. . . . There is a blessing in God writing a new story."[18]

But God is particularly good at working in the midst of the mess. And there's something that happens when I allow myself to be pushed beyond my limits—when we as a couple say yes to new adventures from God that stretch and grow our dependence on Him and on each other.

Adventuring together is part of a thriving relationship. Even when it includes walking through a not-so-easy part of the story. Give it some time to turn out well. Something remarkable happens within us when we choose to trust that He is just as much God in the messy middle as He is at the triumphant ending. God is the God of the long haul. New life *is* coming. There is so much happening underneath the surface. Trust the process. Trust God to work through the power of consistency. Remember, wave upon wave upon wave smooths the stone.

Often over the years, the times I have felt the closest to Chris were during specific seasons where we were forced to rely on one another to make it to the other side of something new. There's a special bond that's formed only on the other side of experiencing a great adventure together. If you've ever gone on an adventure with someone, you know exactly what I'm talking about. Even the hard, messy middle of it provides great reward for our relationship. Even when we can't see it—maybe especially when we can't see it—God is growing something beautiful beneath the surface.

God is growing something beautiful beneath the surface.

AT THE END OF THE DAY

No matter the season, I want to be a spouse who says yes to adventure. Who refuses to rust out. Who continues to push away from the dock of comfort to discover what's waiting out on the open horizon. To live fully awake and alive and spark that sense of adventure in my partner, as well. To stay awake and alive together.

A life of adventure doesn't have to mean hanging off a cliff every day (although I suppose it can). It means that we commit to each other not to fall asleep to our own lives, to care about the flourishing of each other's souls, and to support each other's dreams, as they shift and change along the way. It means our lives are filled with the good stuff of life, the stuff that energizes us, propels us forward, and sparks curiosity. It means stepping in and showing up to the moments of our life—not just skimming through it, but living fully present to all of it, saying yes to new experiences, new adventures, and new opportunities at every turn.

Choose adventure together. Watch your marriage come alive.

—————— PRACTICE

- When's the last time you felt completely alive?

- When's the last time you took a risk together?

- This week, ask your spouse what some of their deepest dreams are. Think of some ways you can begin to water their dreams and watch them grow.

- Brainstorm with your spouse a handful of new things you've each been wanting to try. Make it a goal to try at least one per week.

- Think back over your life together. Are there any difficult seasons you can clearly see now where God was working things out for your good? Discuss with your spouse, and offer a prayer of thanks to the Lord for His faithfulness.

8

FRESH EYES

The Rhythm of Staying in Awe

The whole earth is filled with awe at your wonders;
where morning dawns, where evening fades,
you call forth songs of joy.

PSALM 65:8

Life without wonder is not worth living. What we lack
is not a will to believe but a will to wonder.

ABRAHAM JOSHUA HESCHEL

CHRIS

I've always been the early riser in our house. Most mornings you can find me in the office, sitting in my gray chair, black coffee in hand as I wait for my family to stir. This daily rhythm before all the kids wake up, before the patter of little feet resounds on the stairs, before lunches and backpacks head out the door to school—this daily morning hour helps set the tone for the entire day.

Generally speaking, with five kids, moments of quiet are

hard to come by, so early mornings are when I find them. I love my morning time, reading my Bible, trying to stay off my phone, clearing the distractions, and just being in the moment.

One of my favorite parts of this morning rhythm is when Jenni comes strolling down the stairs, usually still in her pj's, seeking out her first sip of coffee for the day. It never ceases to amaze me, I swear—every single time, my breath catches. I can't help but stop and stare, just in awe of that woman as she walks down the stairs. She literally takes my breath away. As much as I like the initial quiet of the morning, it's this moment, this rhythm I look forward to most every single day. When I see her coming down those steps, I just can't help but think, *Wow! That woman is* my *wife!*

Over the last seventeen years, throughout our marriage, there have been countless times where awe has caught me by surprise and overwhelmed my heart. I think about the five times she's given our family a beautiful baby, and I watched in awe at her strength. I think of the time when we lost a baby through miscarriage, and I watched in awe at how she grieved and sought the Lord. I think of the times I've completely messed up and made huge mistakes, and she loves me, forgives me, and continuously supports me. Or the many times when I've come around the corner to find her all snuggled up on the couch, reading to our girls, attempting flips on the trampoline with our middle schooler, or shooting hoops in the driveway with our teenage son. Those are the moments that take my breath away, and I am awestruck all over again, overwhelmingly grateful for this woman I get to call mine and the life we get to build together.

THE POWER OF AWE

Every morning that we wake up we have a choice. We can enjoy the day or barely survive it. We can choose to view our spouse as the remarkable gift we've been given or as just a fixed part of our ordinary life. We can receive each day with joy and gratitude as a fresh opportunity to know and discover them more or believe the lie that we already know all there is to know of them. The choice is ours. Awe is about how we see. Thriving couples choose to see the world with fresh eyes of awe and wonder.

Awe is defined as gratitude, joy, wonder. A deep sense of admiration and inspiration. It shatters your expectations, it does not lend itself to easy classification, it automatically stops us in our tracks and takes our breath away. As Mark Foreman says, "Whether it's going for a walk on the beach or through the woods, taking in a glowing sunset, or looking at how a parent is loving their newborn, those are all moments of wonder where I realize, there's still magic in the world, because God made this world, and it re-ignites me."[1]

Some things are true whether we believe them or not.[2] Life *is* a stunning miracle. Marriage *is* a beautiful gift, whether we choose to see it or not. Thriving couples keep choosing, over and over, to see the gift of life together for the precious miracle that it truly is, continually reigniting a deep sense of gratitude and curiosity for the magic of life all around them. When we choose to practice this rhythm of awe, the world around us becomes a place of thrilling beauty to be discovered. As Abraham Joshua Heschel wrote, "Our goal should be to live life in radical amazement . . . [to] get up in the morning and look at the world in a way that takes nothing for granted. Everything is phenomenal; every-thing is incredible; never treat life casually. To be spiritual is to be amazed."

Day by day, as we choose to practice seeing the world in this miraculous way, we find our ordinary transformed into extraor-dinary. We discover magic right in the middle of our mundane. The starry night sky, the sunset lighting the clouds on fire, my gorgeous wife walking down the stairs in her pj's each morning. What before seemed normal becomes divine when I allow God to open my eyes to see the beauty within it.

In his book *Contagious*, marketing professor Jonah Berger examined why some articles are shared more than others—what makes one article go viral and not another. What he discovered through his research was, "Awe increases sharing, while sadness decreases it."[3] In each viral article, there's an experience of awe and wonder felt by the reader that compels them to share it with the world.

Awe is something set deep within each of us, something we were born to experience on a regular basis. It waits, ready to be awakened. As Ecclesiastes 3:11 tells us, "[God] has planted eternity in the human heart." Without regular doses of awe, our souls can actually begin to wither. As Albert Einstein noted, "The most beautiful emotion we can experience is the mysteri-ous. . . . He to whom this emotion is a stranger, who can no longer pause to wonder and stand rapt in awe, is as good as dead."[4] If we lose our sense of awe or admiration for each other, we're headed quickly toward disaster. We were made for awe, for life, and to revel in deep gratitude for the great gift of it all: of life, of relationship, of each other.

When we experience awe, it humbles and grounds us. When

we stand in awe of God, for example, in wonder and amazement of who He is, it corrects our view of ourselves, reminding us of how small we are in relation to Someone so much bigger and greater. Awe adjusts our perspective. Researcher and professor Dr. Dacher Keltner notes,

> Even brief experiences of awe, such as being amid beautiful tall trees, lead people to feel less narcissistic and entitled and more attuned to the common humanity people share with one another. In the great balancing act of our social lives, between the gratification of self-interest and a concern for others, fleeting experiences of awe redefine the self in terms of the collective, and orient our actions toward the needs of those around us.[5]

When we cultivate a sense of awe, or admiration and deep gratitude for our spouse, it corrects the way we view them. It cultivates humility within us and rids us of any sense of entitlement. Practicing awe reminds us that they do not belong to us, they belong to God, and we are accountable not only to them but also to Him for the way we choose to treat them. It reminds us that they are a child of God just as we are, with transcendent value and worth—a gift to be treasured, not a burden to bear.

Looking for awe in our everyday life together also helps us see the remarkable value in the marriage we're building. It enables us to tread more lightly as we work through areas of conflict. It resets our priorities as we remember how fast it all goes by, and that the work we're doing in our marriage and in our life together is truly important work.

Awe also protects us from becoming blind to the magic of

life all around us. It gives us a different lens to see our spouse. Awe is about cultivating a heart of overwhelming gratitude for the unbelievable gift of getting to love someone. It keeps us curious and leaning into their life, asking questions, seeking to know more and more of who they are and who they are becoming in each new season. What a tragedy to think, *I already know all there is to know about you.* With each new season, just as we are, they are growing and changing and becoming someone new. I want to know that new person, and I want to be a helpful part of their journey of becoming. No one else gets to do that for them; God chose me. What a gift!

LEVELS OF AWE

JENNI

Now, of course, there are different levels of awe and admiration. I think it's important to clarify, we are not suggesting for a moment that we should worship our spouse in the same way that we worship God. There is a level of awe in our response to the presence of God that no earthly thing can touch. This "great awe" is reserved for God and God alone, for what Tim Keller calls the worship of "ultimate things."[6] But there is also a healthy sense of awe and wonder that God gives us as we encounter His creation—whether it's our spouse, a newborn baby, a rushing waterfall, or a majestic sunset. These experiences of awe do not replace the wonder we have for the Creator of these experiences but instead point our hearts back to Him, with gratitude for the only true source of so much beauty and life.

What was your first encounter of awe? There are certain experiences in life that leave you awestruck forever. I remember a particular season, years ago, in those wonderfully awkward middle school years, of just beginning to grapple with my faith. For the first time, the summer of my seventh-grade year, my relationship with Jesus became real to me in a new way. I don't know how else to describe it other than to say I had an encounter with Him. In the middle of a sweaty camp in Columbus, Texas. I felt the undeniable presence of God for the very first time, and I was never the same.

I never got over it. It was my first experience of great awe. That rush of joy, peace, wonder, gratitude, all wrapped up into one emotion. I just remember thinking, *I could stay here forever.* This encounter of awe with God also changed the sense of awe I was able to have for those He put around me. Somehow, adoring Him enabled me to more easily adore the people He placed in my life. This is the power of awe.

A LIFETIME OF AWE
CHRIS

I recently landed a consulting gig with a company in New York City and found myself in a get-to-know-you conversation with the client. She's in the publishing space and was trying to build a new subscription business. As I was listening to her, trying to find the elements of her story to build her brand around, we found ourselves down the side-road topic of marriage.

She was aware of my long, happy marriage with Jenni and that we have five kids (a few of the kids had run in on our Zoom meetings from time to time, thanks to working from home during the coronavirus pandemic). But as we dove into the topic of marriage, this young, influential entrepreneur began to tell me her view on marriage, which mirrors that of people in the world around her. She wasn't quite sure, she said, that she really wanted to be with just one person for her whole life. To her and others in her generation, that seemed extremely old-fashioned.

She mentioned a conversation she'd recently had with a man who also lived in the heart of New York City. In this world of dating apps, he said that he could literally go on a different date every night with someone new, that he could hear different stories, hit different restaurants, and potentially hook up with a different person, no strings attached.

I could hear the tension in her voice and see the undecided expression on her face as she shared this story. On the one hand, she had talked herself into thinking this was pretty cool and very in-line with the times, but on the other hand, there was a level of disappointment in her voice, and her face had a flat expression. Her words were saying she agreed, but a different feeling lurked underneath.

As she finished, she looked at me and asked, "So, why would anyone want to settle down with just one person for the rest of their *life*?" My answer came easily. I said, "I've experienced the opposite of what you just shared. I am married to someone who knows all of me, my strengths and my weaknesses. She has seen me at my absolute worst and at my very best. We've grown up together, wrestled through incredibly difficult seasons together, and come out stronger on the other side of it. There is no one on this planet who knows me better than Jenni Graebe, and the amazing thing is, even knowing all of my many flaws, she still chooses me every single day and loves me unconditionally. And after seventeen years of marriage to this one incredible woman, I can guarantee you that a one-night stand has *nothing* on the life we've built together and the love that we share. Not even close. And that's why someone would choose to give their heart to just one person for the rest of their life."

She didn't say anything in response, and she didn't have to. Maybe speaking that truth out loud was more for me then it was for her—but this truly is the embodiment of the rhythm of awe. If we aren't careful, we can look across the laundry list that is our marriage—kids, vacations, job changes, home projects—and think it's all routine. But the truth is, marriage is a miracle, and each step we take together should be a reminder of awe. Two individuals who have the capability of being selfish have instead chosen to fall in step with another person. They've turned their eyes toward their spouse and committed to keep discovering them, growing with them, and celebrating them for a lifetime. Marriage is a miracle, and the more we stop to remember that, the closer we move toward the relationship we long for.

Marriage is a miracle.

LOSING AWE

JENNI ──────────────────────────────

How do we lose our sense of awe, and how can we guard against that happening? Let's look at some important ruts to avoid as we seek to practice this rhythm of awe.

The Myth of the Ordinary

We cannot let the great gift of marriage become ordinary. When our relationship with our spouse loses its luster, we can forget its incredible value. Hindsight is 20/20. What a great tragedy it would be if it were only after it's all said and done that we finally wake up to realize what golden days we were living in.

When it's all over, what we wouldn't give to go back, just for one day, to spend one afternoon with those young, passionate twentysomethings who couldn't keep their hands off each other.

Or when our kids are grown and gone, what we wouldn't give to go back for just one pancake-Saturday morning with those toddlers jumping all around us, hot cups of coffee steaming, glorious toddler lisps and the sweetest bed heads surrounding us. We don't know what we have till it's gone—*unless* we pay attention. **Unless we pursue awe.** When we choose to look for things to be awed by in marriage, when we look at our spouse with anticipation and a sense of discovery, we free our marriage from the lie of the ordinary and the danger it brings.

I'll never forget another favorite interview we had on the show with *New York Times*–bestselling author Gary Thomas. We enjoyed a wonderful, rich conversation with Gary and at the very end, he stopped us and offered this encouragement to us and other young couples listening who were deep in the throes of raising young kids. He said, "Hey, if God were to come to my wife and I today and say, 'I'll give you a month all expenses paid in Europe, Michelin three-star restaurants, five-star hotels, go wherever you want—*or* you can have a weekend when your kids were seven, five, and two, when you lived in that little townhouse in Virginia, with the car that died if you turned too sharp on right turns, and your biggest expenditure was a Blockbuster movie rental on Friday night while you did laundry and the kids slept,' Lisa and I wouldn't even look at each other—we would say, 'Please, please—Let us go back for that one weekend!' So I know it's hard," he said, "and I know it's exhausting when you have young kids, but they are truly glorious years. . . . and you'll miss them when they're gone."[7]

We've recalled that encouragement from Gary many times since then, as the exhaustion attempts to blind us from the glory of the season we're in. The greatest gift, of course, is for us to practice living daily from that place of awe and gratitude. To remind ourselves of the truth: *There is no such thing as ordinary.*

What a gift. To be entrusted with a human to love for a lifetime. What would we change about the way we lived our life together if we began to view our spouse in this way? What if we remembered how quickly time goes by, and what a wonderful privilege it is to wake up next to them each morning? How would it change the way we treat them? What would be our next move?

If you're in the middle of what feels like an ordinary season in your marriage—if you're stuck in the ruts—imagine yourself at the end of your life. What are the golden moments you'll remember fondly from this time? What do you think you'll miss someday? Remind yourself of the good and beautiful things your spouse brings into the world—the way she always seems to have the insight you need when you're stuck, the way he brings laughter into serious moments. Thriving couples shut down the myth of ordinary by choosing awe. They choose gratitude, choose to see and be thankful for the good, and continually shift back toward each other. In little and big ways, step-by-step, choice by choice we can begin to grow a deep sense of admiration for our spouse that will carry us through the toughest of times. At the end of the day, "happiness is not having what you want but wanting what you have."[8] Thriving couples dispel the myth of ordinary by choosing awe.

> Thriving couples dispel the myth of ordinary by choosing awe.

The Problem of Contempt

One of the greatest dangers to a thriving relationship—and a thief of awe—is contempt. In fact, according to research psychologist Dr. John Gottman, contempt is the number-one predictor of divorce in couples. "When contempt begins to overwhelm your relationship you tend to forget entirely your partner's positive qualities, at least while you're feeling upset. You can't remember a single positive quality or act. This *immediate decay of admiration* is an important reason why contempt ought to be banned from marital interactions."[9]

Dr. Gottman found that the most successful couples he observed entered a state of mind called "positive sentiment override," where they have built such a strong bond with each other—through practicing habits like verbal gratitude, enjoying real connection, and developing admiration of each other—that they can more easily settle conflicts, let go of minor annoyances, and make greater allowances for each other's faults. The couples who did not cultivate a strong bond with each other fell into a place of "negative sentiment override," finding it harder not to become frustrated and annoyed by minor problems and noticing that even the smallest issues could set them off.[10]

In other words, when we're not practicing the rhythm of awe, along with the other rhythms we've learned in previous chapters, we are more easily set off when conflict comes. When we neglect to cultivate eyes to see our spouse and what they offer as a gift, we can start to view them instead as a problem. Everything seems like a personal attack, even minor offenses, and we become blind to the many positive aspects of our relationship, even though they are all around us. Contempt blinds us from seeing the good in each other.

If you find yourself in a place of contempt with your spouse, take heart, friend. We are all always one choice away from moving back in the right direction. We can start today. Thriving couples banish contempt by choosing awe. When the emotional connection with each other is strong, we see more easily the positive aspects of our spouse, let go of offenses more quickly, and have a strong relationship to lean on when conflict comes.

The Thief of Comparison and Entitlement

Another great danger of awe is entitlement. Over time in marriage, we can start to believe the great lie that our spouse belongs to us. When we think our spouse is a fixed part of our life, we can begin to take them for granted. We forget that waking up next to them every morning is not, in fact, a given. We lose our curiosity for their life, to know more of who they are, and what God's doing in them. Awe cannot exist alongside entitlement because entitlement robs us of the ability to be grateful. Entitlement says, *There is always more I deserve, and you are never enough.*

A close brother to entitlement—and another thief of awe—is comparison. Comparison is a poison that blinds us to the abundant blessings all around us. As Dr. Henry Cloud says, "People who are motivated by envy define the good as that which I don't have."[11] Envy keeps us constantly looking over our shoulder at what those around us possess, convincing us that somehow it must be so much better than what we have. The grass is always greener on the other side. But the truth is, our yard has the same potential to be just as flourishing as our neighbors', if we choose to water and care for it.

The Wound of Unforgiveness

Sometimes the thief of awe is deep pain and unforgiveness. I want to stop and acknowledge here that some parts of our stories hold deep wounds. Hateful words have been spoken. Hopes and dreams have died. Needs have been neglected. Pain is real, and it's important to recognize where we've been hurt and share honestly about it with our spouse. Our marriage cannot thrive if we ignore or deny where we've been wounded. When the air is calm and emotions aren't running the show, take some time to be open and honest with your spouse about where you've been hurt. Acknowledging the truth is always the beginning of healing. Remember, true change begins with honesty.

The goal in bringing deep pain and unforgiveness to the surface is not to point our finger at our partner's faults, even in an effort to help them. The goal is always forgiveness and reconciliation. Forgiveness does not negate the wrong done to us, but it does free us to move forward into a better tomorrow. Forgiveness enables us to see once again through the lens of awe and wonder and opens us up to create the marriage we long for.

> Forgiveness does not negate the wrong done to us, but it does free us to move forward into a better tomorrow.

Eugene Peterson said, "All suffering, all pain, all emptiness, all disappointment is seed: sow it in God and he will, finally, bring a crop of joy from it."[12] Forgiveness can restore awe by opening our eyes once again to see our spouse as a blessing, rather than clinging to and defining them by the hurts of the past. If we allow Him to, God can teach us His kind of compassion that frees others in our lives to be defined by who they are in Him, rather than their mistakes that may have wounded us.

MINDSET MATTERS

To be clear, we are not calling for a return to viewing life and marriage as a sentimental fairy tale. Far from it. Like anything truly meaningful and valuable in life, a thriving marriage requires a lot of work and sacrifice. But here comes the point: It's worth it. As the great theologian Jimmy Dugan said in the famous baseball classic, "The hard is what makes it great."[13] The hard is not what makes it miserable. The hard—the work, the sacrifice, the pouring out of ourselves for the benefit of another—is what makes it great. The work of choosing to speak words of encouragement rather than pointing out their faults. The work of getting up early to make them a cup of coffee. The work of choosing them over the world's myriad of distractions. The work of refusing to let the worries of life blind us to the gift of it all, that's work that's worth it.

Marriage is hard, yes. This is a true statement. This is not, however, a helpful perspective to live from. Not the empowering mindset that will lead us to the thriving marriage we long for. While "marriage is hard" may be true, it is not the whole truth; never a good place to stop and set up camp. Just as my identity in Christ is not that I am a terrible sinner . . . but rather that I am loved by Him and made new in Him. To live fully and joyfully requires I shift my mindset. Likewise, to have a thriving marriage requires that we move beyond the "marriage is hard" mindset and move toward "marriage is a gift" to be cherished and enjoyed.

PRACTICING AWE

To bend the will, you first must change the heart.

SANDRA McCRACKEN

So how do we begin to cultivate awe as a daily practice? How do we integrate touchpoints of this rhythm into our marriage? The truth is, every single day, all around us are endless opportunities for awe. If we practice noticing, practice offering our deepest gratitude, pray for eyes to see the extraordinary wrapped up in the ordinary, it will lead us to see life in a whole new way, to see our partner in a new way, as someone we just can't help but marvel at.

What are some practical ways we can pull out the extraordinary from our ordinary?

Live a Life of Gratitude

One of the great restorers of awe is gratitude. As author Francis Frangipane says, "The very quality of your life, whether you love it or hate it, is based on how thankful you are toward God. Your attitude determines whether life to you is a place of blessedness or wretchedness . . . it all depends on your perspective."[14] What we're talking about here is not just a general, occasional sense of thankfulness but rather building a true sense of awe and gratitude for our spouse by intentionally searching out and giving thanks for the blessings they add to our life. Frangipane continues, "If you want to find joy, you must first find thankfulness. . . . The fact is, every time we open up to grumbling and complaining, the quality of our life is reduced proportionately."[15]

Practicing gratitude opens the door for the marriage we dream of. Each time we go out of our way to discover something positive about our spouse, each time we pause to offer a silent thanks for the gift we've been given, we are working to build a culture of appreciation, joy, and love where a strong relationship can grow. The more we practice looking for awe, the more we develop eyes to see it.

The key to staying in awe is to remember it's all a gift. This man, this woman standing in front of you is a great gift to be treasured, not a burden to bear. Twenty years from now, you will give anything to go back and live this day over again, just one more time. To soak up one more moment with this blessing right in front of you. We create a culture of awe in our marriage when we choose to cherish and esteem our spouse—in big and small ways.

> The key to staying in awe is to remember it's all a gift.

Look for Magic

Another restorer of awe is celebration—looking for magic in the middle of the mundane; going out of our way to find seemingly small things to celebrate. Reasons to celebrate are all around us, all the time, if we choose to see them. Abraham Joshua Heschel wrote, "[People] of our time [are] losing the power of celebration. Instead of celebrating, [we seek] to be amused or entertained. Celebration is an active state, an act of expressing reverence or appreciation. . . . Celebration is a confrontation, giving attention to the transcendent meaning of one's actions."[16]

It happened to Chris and me just this morning, over a plate of jelly toast with our toddler. We found awe right in the thick of a sleepy breakfast chat, in striped pajamas and silly morning giggles from this extraordinary kid. In every precious, mispro-nounced word that tumbled out of her mouth, even the whiny ones. And in the reminder that we are living in the golden years, a season that will be over before we know it.

It happened last week when a glimpse of Chris playing tag with our daughter in the backyard stopped me in my tracks. What I have found is that choosing to pause whatever I am doing long enough to acknowledge those glimpses of awe is like making a deposit in my awe tank. Over time, each one of these moments adds up to transform my heart and overall attitude toward my spouse and toward the life we are building together. When hard moments come, as they always do, I have a sizable account of joy to lean on.

> Magic is all around us every day. Ask God for eyes to see it.

Magic is all around us every day. Ask God for eyes to see it. It could be a starry sky, the way the light hits your child's face, catching your spouse's eye in a meaningful moment together, savoring your favorite activity together. The sky is the limit. Each moment where we choose awe matters. May we savor each one and stoke the fire of awe for the beautiful gifts of life and of each other.

Pray

There is nothing more powerful than praying for what you lack. Talk about extraordinary masquerading as ordinary. We have been given access to the Creator of the universe, the Lord of all the earth, and most days, we pass prayer off as our last resort. Pray for eyes to see the awe, to see the extraordinary in your spouse. Before you go to bed each night, take just a moment to pray together, reflecting on the moments of your day with gratitude. Offer thanks together for the gift of each other and ask for strength to take the lessons learned today into all that awaits you tomorrow.[17]

Take an Awe Walk Together

Yes, this is an actual thing. Just in case your spouse may call this a hippy, granola activity (ask me how I know), here is scientific research to further your cause. In a study conducted at the University of California–Berkley, a group of participants who spent time gazing at trees in nature were contrasted with a group who spent time gazing at buildings. The study concluded that "those who focused on the trees felt more awe and later were more likely to help a person in need, show greater ethical decision-making, and report less feelings of superiority to others."[18]

In an article for *Psychology Today*, Dr. Bryan E. Robinson elaborates on the implications of taking an awe walk: "In an awe state . . . you're engaged with the expansiveness of the external world, less focused on yourself and more on others, which takes your mind off your burdens, trials and tribulations, your worries, anxieties and frustrations."[19]

So, leave your phone behind, grab your spouse, and head to the prettiest trails you can find. As you walk together, intentionally take in the beauty of God's creation around you. Take a deep breath, smell the fresh scents of the trees. Awe walks have been scientifically proven to lift your mood, ease your worries, and draw you closer to one another.[20]

Enjoy Each Other

As we may have mentioned a few times, the point of this rhythm is to view marriage as a great gift from God. And as Tyler Staton says, "There is no better response to a gift giver than to enjoy the gift. There is no sweeter worship than to enjoy the life He has given you to live."[21] We serve a God who enjoys us and even delights in us (see Psalm 18:19). When we delight in each other, it brings Him—and us—great joy. Don't take yourselves too seriously. Stay playful. Enjoy one another. Delighting in one another and in the life we get to share lightens the load. What do you love to do together? What activities reignite your love for each other? How can you proactively make room in your life to enjoy them more often?

One way to restore an immediate sense of awe and joy toward our spouse is to imagine how empty life would be without them. As writer and philosopher G. K. Chesterton said, "The way to love anything is to realize that it might be lost."[22] There's a healthy kind of fear that comes from making a habit of awe a part of our lives. It's a reverent fear that reminds us that our days with our spouse are numbered, and the truth is, we don't know how many we will have. Practicing awe in this way inspires me to make the most of each day we are given together—enjoying whatever time we have together in this life.

Sex

CHRIS ————————————————————————————————

Let's talk about sex, shall we? Here we are in the rhythm of awe, and I think it would be a darn shame if we didn't carve out some real estate here to talk about sex. (And if the classic Salt-N-Pepa song "Let's Talk About Sex" just began playing in your head, well—you and I are kindred spirits.) One of my favorite things to talk about (and, let's be honest, to do) is sex. Now, I realize this topic can quickly become a hornet's nest, but hornet's nests have never bothered me one bit. So let's go for it.

Those close to Jenni and me know I tend to be an over-sharer. Through the years, Jenni has graciously helped me learn where the line is when it comes to divulging details of our personal life. So much so that she wisely advised me early in our marriage, "If you think to yourself, *Maybe I shouldn't say this*, you definitely shouldn't." She knows that for whatever reason, my privacy filter was just never coded correctly, and if *I'm* thinking maybe I shouldn't say it, then it's *100-percent* a nonsharing moment for me. So, with all that said, I'm going to be super respectful of our personal life and listen to that little voice of wisdom when it comes to talking about sex.

We, like all couples, have had our own journey toward healthy intimacy, working through the great and not-so-great things we both brought along with us into our marriage. We've had years and years of growing together on this journey toward rediscovering the beauty and gift that is sex.

My absolute favorite place in the whole entire world is lying next to my wife before we make love. Of course, the anticipation of the physical enjoyment is great, but it's become so much more than that for me. Those moments of quiet, of waiting, are sacred, a suspended time of complete awe where the world's most beautiful woman—who brought five amazing kids into this world, who loves me through all my faults—has once again chosen to say yes to me. To say yes to one of the most trusting, vulnerable, and beautiful moments that God has ever created. I'm in awe of how God created this way for me and my wife to connect beyond words.

Sex is one of God's greatest gifts. No matter how many years we've been together, we should always be intentional to make sure that we're still pursuing and enjoying one another. Recently I shared with a friend that sex is just as much a spiritual and emotional experience as it is physical. Do you believe that? Maybe you've never thought about it that way, but it's crucial that we understand this side of sex. Early in the book we talked about ruts. One of the areas we can easily find ourselves in a rut is in the bedroom. I've heard so many stories of couples who haven't had sex for months or years, and that breaks my heart. Others might be engaging in sex more regularly, but if they are honest, it's more out of routine than it is out of passion, and they definitely aren't experiencing many moments of awe.

Take a step back with God. Check your heart and ask yourself, *When was the last time I viewed sex as an opportunity for awe?* What would it look like for you to take the opportunity to look in wonder at your spouse, to see sex not as a chore or duty but as a gift and a miracle every time you both say yes to each other?

The couples who enjoy the healthiest sex lives are those who are able to talk openly about it together. It's impossible to move toward thriving in this area if we're completely unaware of what a healthy version of intimacy looks like for our spouse. I'm not here to tell you how often you should have sex. But what I can tell you is that it's an important conversation to have with your spouse. Each of us has our own vision for what great intimacy looks like, and usually it differs greatly from that of our partner.

So the goal here is to truly get to know our spouse in this area. Again, change will only occur to the degree we are willing to be honest. What turns our spouse off, and what turns them on? What feels comfortable to them, and what doesn't? How many times a week feels like a healthy amount to them and to you? If you've never actually had this conversation with your spouse, there's no better time than the present. Uncovering what both of your dreams and desires are is the first step to moving toward a thriving sex life.

AT THE END OF THE DAY

I want to pray like crazy for the incredible human I get to call mine for however long God deems possible—and for the life we share. I want to view our life together as the miracle that it truly is. I want to stay in awe of the gift of loving someone for a lifetime. I want to remember that being entrusted with someone to love is a gift. I want to live and love from *that* place, to choose to see my spouse as a tremendous blessing to cherish instead of a burden to bear. And I want to be awake and alive to it all.

May we choose every day to practice the rhythm of awe, and may it change the way we see our spouse and the great gift of life together. A shared life is a miracle. We thrive when we stay in awe of our spouse and of the gift of loving someone for a lifetime. When we live and love from *that* place, we'll find our marriage coming awake and alive.

PRACTICE

- Start a gratitude journal of things you notice about your spouse.

- Send your spouse a quick text every morning or evening with just one thing you're thankful for about them.

- Take an awe walk together through a tree-lined trail.

- Pray for eyes to see the magic hidden in the middle of the mundane. Make a goal to find at least one moment of awe every day.

- Create an awe playlist of songs that transport you to experience awe.

- Is there a specific place that evokes awe and wonder for you and your spouse? Hang a picture, quote, or souvenir from that place somewhere in your home so you will see it every day.

PART THREE

FINDING YOUR UNIQUE RHYTHMS

AS WE TALKED ABOUT in the beginning of this book, we already have a "rhythm of us," whether we realize it or not—the collection of habits we choose to fill our lives with on a regular basis. The question is, do we like where our rhythm is taking us? Do we like the couple it's shaping us to become? The truth is, the rhythms we create in our life and in our marriage now will determine the couple we become in the future.

Chances are, you already have consistent rhythms in place, rhythms that affect you both more than you realize. In this section, we'll move toward awareness by naming the habits that carry us. Maybe you kiss her on the forehead every morning as you head out the door for work. Maybe she always brings you a nice, cold glass of lemonade when you're mowing the grass. Maybe he whips up a stack of his famous pancakes and bacon every Saturday morning. Naming these life-giving rhythms allows us to see their significance and motivates us to prioritize them more intentionally.

The rhythms we create in our life and in our marriage now will determine the couple we become in the future.

Similarly, there are likely at least a few unhealthy habits you'll want to become aware of so you can keep them from becoming a regular part of your rhythm. Maybe you find yourself on the phone a little too much during dinnertime. Maybe the TV has been on way too much during vital time to connect in the evenings. Examining our habits helps us become aware of things that might be pulling us away from each other and the life we want to create.

As you look back on your time spent together over the last few days, weeks, and months, consider the rhythms that bring you the most life and those that don't, the habits that draw you closer to one another and those that distance you. Creating a rhythm of us is a powerful way to intentionally strengthen those habits that bring us life, joy, and connection, moving us—over time—to build a life and marriage that takes our breath away.

9

UNCOVER
YOUR VALUES

Naming What Matters Most

We must pay the most careful attention, therefore,
to what we have heard, so that we do not drift away.

HEBREWS 2:1

OUR RHYTHMS EMERGE out of what we value. That's why, when the rhythms that fill our life and marriage flow from our deepest shared values, we experience the thriving marriage we long for. Take some time to make a list of what matters most to you, individually, and then together as a couple. Talk through any important values in your life you may have drifted from. Work to identify what things make you come alive, personally and together. What do you hope to be *known for* as a person? As a couple? Write down anything that comes to mind. This is just for you.

Reflect together on any areas of your life that continually cause conflict and stress in your marriage. What value could they be pointing to? Write it down. Reach out to a few thriving couples in your life and ask what their highest values are. What do they refuse to tolerate in their lives? Write it all down here. Be as specific as you can. Writing things down helps signal our brains to pay attention to and remember things we value.[1] Don't worry about getting it perfect or final—this is just about naming what matters most to you.

WHAT MATTERS MOST

What activities make you come alive personally?

....

....

....

....

What do you hope to be known for as a person?

....

....

....

....

Are there any areas of your life together that continually cause you joy? What value could the joy be pointing to?

....

....

....

....

Think of a couple whose relationship inspires you. What are some of their highest values?

....

....

....

....

Which activities make you feel alive and fulfilled when you share them with your spouse?

....

....

....

....

What do you hope to be known for as a couple?

....

....

....

....

Are there any areas of your life together that continually cause you issues and stress? What value could the frustration be pointing to?

....

....

....

....

In the middle portion of this book, we identified five healthy rhythms, each of which emerges from specific values. We speak life because we value creating a culture of honor and respect. We serve because we value a life of caring for others. We slow down because we value meaningful connection. We seek adventure because we value staying awake and alive to our life. We stay in awe because we value seeing life as a beautiful gift.

With that in mind, reflect back on the rhythms you've identified as key to your marriage, and take a minute to identify the values those reflect. Underneath each value, jot down a few intentional ways you could begin to practice them in your daily or weekly life together. For example, if you named the value of staying in awe, your practices might look like this:

- Begin each day by writing down three things you're grateful for in your spouse.
- Set aside ten minutes to reflect on the day together and name the moments worth celebrating.
- End each day in reflective prayer together.

VALUE: ....

    PRACTICE: ....

    ....

    ....

    ....

    ....

    ....

VALUE: ....

    PRACTICE: ....

    ....

    ....

    ....

    ....

    ....

VALUE: ....

    PRACTICE: ....

    ....

    ....

    ....

    ....

    ....

VALUE: ....

PRACTICE: ....

....

....

....

....

....

VALUE: ....

PRACTICE: ....

....

....

....

....

....

Remember, there are a thousand different ways we could choose to live our life together. We move toward the thriving life and marriage we long for when we intentionally center our lives around the values and rhythms that lead us toward God and toward each other.

10

UNCOVER YOUR RHYTHM

Moving Toward Life-Giving Habits

ᴼNCE WE UNDERSTAND our shared values as a couple, we're able to better evaluate our unique rhythms as a couple. To do this, we keep our values in mind as we take a detailed inventory about what we want to prioritize, what we want to improve, and what we want to let go of. Because we are individuals, with our own patterns and choices, we first start by considering our personal rhythms—because those rhythms affect the person we share life with. Then we consider our rhythms as a couple, the habits and ways of living that we've developed together. Once we've done that, we can decide together how we want to handle these rhythms moving forward.

What does "a day in the life" look like for you?

....

....

....

....

....

....

....

What does "a day in the life" look like for your spouse?

....

....

....

....

....

....

....

Which rhythms bring you joy?

....

....

....

....

Which interactions drain your energy?

....

....

....

....

Which rhythms are already working well for you?

....

....

....

....

Which interactions lift your spirits?

....

....

....

....

Which rhythms cause you to come alive and feel more like the person you long to be?

....
....
....
....

Which rhythms stir your heart for God?

....
....
....
....

Which rhythms move you away from the person you want to be?

....
....
....
....

Which rhythms pull you away from God?

....
....
....
....

Which habits are carrying you well in this season? Why?

....

....

....

....

Which habits are not working for you in this season? Why?

....

....

....

....

Are there any activities missing from your day that you'd like to create space for?

....

....

....

....

Are there any rhythms that almost work, but need improving in some way?

....

....

....

....

TOGETHER INVENTORY

Which rhythms create meaningful connection with your spouse?

....

....

....

....

Which rhythms align most with your highest values as a couple?

....

....

....

....

Which rhythms draw you closer to each other?

....

....

....

....

Which rhythms are carrying you well as a couple?

....

....

....

....

Which habits cause negative distance or friction between you and your spouse?

....

....

....

....

Which rhythms distract from your highest priorities as a couple?

....

....

....

....

Which rhythms pull you away from each other?

....

....

....

....

Which rhythms no longer fit the life you want to create together?

....

....

....

....

PULLING IT ALL TOGETHER

Rhythms worth prioritizing:

....

....

....

....

Rhythms worth keeping and improving:

....

....

....

....

Rhythms worth letting go of to make space for what truly matters:

....

....

....

....

UNCOVER
YOUR VISION

Imagining the Future You

I can take you where you want to go....
Dance with me, I want to be your partner,
Can't you see?

ORLEANS

AT THE VERY BEGINNING of this journey, you spent some time dreaming about the future you—the hopes and dreams you and your spouse brought to this book together. Now that you've explored the core rhythms and thought through some of your current habits and values, it's time to discuss what those visions look like. Vision is seeing into the future before it exists, and the more we can be aligned on that future, the stronger our marriage will be.

When we come together in marriage, we each have a vision

for what we hope it will be. It may be a vague sense of happiness and security, or it might be something more specific, the pieces of what you've seen in the thriving marriages around you. Naming each of our visions for our life together, and then seeing where they align and differ, allows us to be on the same page so we can work together to move toward where we both want to go. It also allows us to identify the areas of our life that are already in wonderful alignment or close to that vision and where we need some work. Where we're naturally strong, and where we may need some outside help.

Take some time to envision and put into words the life you want to create together. What does your life look like in your wildest dreams? Maybe you've done this before, when you first got married, but it's been a while and your vision has changed. Or maybe you've never actually put words to the life you want at all. Now is your time. Maybe it looks like taking a different career path for him or going back to school for her; maybe it looks like honoring the value of someone staying home with the kids or supporting a dream to become a writer. Where do you dream of living someday? How often do you want to travel together? Have sex? Go on dates? Write it all down.

After you've clearly named your vision, set aside some time to talk through the future you desire. Make it special, if you can. It doesn't have to be fancy—just *intentional*. Make sure you do this in a time where you are free from distraction and won't be interrupted. After the kids are in bed or you're both finished with work for the day, light a candle and pour some wine, or go on a walk through the trees together, and then talk through what your life together looks like in your wildest dreams.

What does your marriage look like in your wildest dreams?

....

....

....

....

....

....

....

What do you want to be true of you as a couple?

....

....

....

....

As you discuss both of your visions for the future you, what areas are alike?

....

....

....

....

What areas are different?

....

....

....

....

Which aspects of your vision are already part of your current life?

....

....

....

....

Which parts of the vision are most important to you in this current season? What are some things you could work on to make them a reality in your life together?

....

....

....

....

Downloads available at: therhythmofus.com.

PUTTING IT ALL TOGETHER

Craft Your Rhythm

If you want to go anywhere, the map is absolutely necessary.

C. S. LEWIS

THIS IS THE FUN PART of the journey, where all your reflecting, uncovering, and dreaming come together to finally encompass your rhythm of life as a couple. Glance back at your list of rhythms to keep, top core values, and vision of the future you. What surfaced as you considered each question? Did anything surprise you? What areas of your vision did you find different than your spouse? What areas were the same?

Maybe you found that you're closer to your vision than you thought, or at least headed in the right direction. Maybe you've found yourself stuck in rhythms you don't want. Now is the time to get unstuck. Prioritize the values of the rhythms over the details.

Finding your rhythm doesn't mean controlling each other but rather protecting your freedom to choose the life you both want. Each of your values can have a place in your collective rhythm.

With time and intentional practice, each of these rhythms can start to become part of the natural flow of life and relationship together. It's important to make intentional space for each value by putting them into the calendar as well as develop a mindset that looks for opportunities to practice them throughout our days. Here we've provided some ideas to get you started as you think through different rhythms that work for you and your spouse. Each of the core rhythms are included, and there's space for you to include the unique rhythms you've identified as well.

SPEAKING LIFE

- *Find one positive thing about your spouse to acknowledge, then take a moment to acknowledge it out loud around the dinner table.*

-

-

-

SERVING

- Surprise your spouse with their favorite breakfast in bed this week.

-

-

-

SLOWING DOWN

- What's something your spouse has been asking to do for a while? Surprise them this week by making it happen. Maybe it's calling a sitter and making reservations at their favorite restaurant, whisking them away for a campout underneath the stars, or even being the one to initiate intimacy.

-

-

-

SEEKING ADVENTURE

- Make it your mission to discover your spouse's dream. Find at least one way to water that dream by helping them bring it to life.

-

-

-

STAYING IN AWE

- Leave your phone behind, grab your spouse and head to the prettiest trails you can find. As you walk together, intentionally take in the beauty of God's creation around you. Take a deep breath, smell the fresh scents of the trees around you. As you walk, notice how it lifts your mood, eases your worries, and draws you closer to one another.

-

-

-

UNIQUE RHYTHM: ....

-

-

-

UNIQUE RHYTHM: ....

-

-

-

UNIQUE RHYTHM: ....

-

-

-

Downloads available at: therhythmofus.com.

EPILOGUE

A

BRAND-NEW DAY

Grace for the Journey

Trust GOD from the bottom of your heart;
don't try to figure out everything on your own.
Listen for GOD's voice in everything you do,
everywhere you go;
he's the one who will keep you on track.

PROVERBS 3:5-6, MSG

THRIVING COUPLES ARE NOT a select group of rare, extraordinary people. Ordinary people move toward a thriving marriage by choosing to practice extraordinary rhythms. These life-changing practices are available to all of us. We can promise you this: When you ground your rhythms in the truth of God's Word and His desire for you and your spouse, they work. Practicing His ways will always lead us to a place that is good, a place we long to be.

But all good things take time. Good growth is always slow growth. Without a doubt, there will be bumps along the way. Just choose a few rhythms at a time and add them to your daily routine. Be as kind as you can toward each other and toward yourself along the way. Most of us will be tempted to give up quickly on something we don't feel good at right away, so when we're stepping out to try some of these new rhythms, it's important not to be too hard on ourselves or on each other. No one starts off an expert at anything. The important thing is to encourage each other, remember our vision for the future us, and don't give up. Today is a brand-new day. You are headed somewhere *good*.

> Let us not become weary in doing good, for at
> the proper time we will reap a harvest if we do not
> give up.
>
> GALATIANS 6:9

As pastor Tom Nelson says, "God is a God of the long haul. Don't base [your] judgment on how things are going according to right now."[1] If you're discouraged about where you are in your relationship as you begin to work on your rhythms, give it some time to turn out well! Just keep going, step-by-step, choice by choice, remembering that the fruit is found in the keeping on. We *will* reap a harvest if we don't give up.

I love what author Erwin McManus says in *The Last Arrow*: "I wonder how many times in my own life I thought that I failed but actually the only thing that happened was that I quit."[2] The only way to fail is to quit. Keep going. Building a life and marriage we love is hard work, but it's worth it!

We can set out with the best of intentions and still be met with roadblocks outside our control. What matters most is how we choose to respond when life doesn't go according to our plans. When you fall down, just get back up. You'll be amazed at the incredible impact your efforts have on your relationship, awkward as they may be at first. Resist the urge to calculate your success based on the perfection with which you practice these rhythms. Success is not measured by finishing our to-do list each day but by the connection we're building with our spouse. That is the harvest we're after.

> The fruit is found in the keeping on.

AS YOU GO

Pray

Start each day with prayer. Stand in great awe of the One who made you, loves you, and is always ready to help as you pursue the thriving life and marriage He has for you. Pray for His strength when you hit a bump along the way. In moments you are tempted to fall into old patterns, pray for His grace to remind you of the new, healthy rhythms you have learned. When you find yourself frustrated and feel like letting your words fly, take a deep breath and pray for the grace to speak words of kindness instead. Ask God to open your eyes to new ways you could serve your spouse. Cherish each moment He's given you together. Lean into His courage as you say yes to those new adventures He's inviting you in to. And offer thanks from the deepest depths of your heart for the unbelievable gift of it all!

Find Community

Seek out other thriving couples in your life. This is crucial. Ask God to surround you with them. We simply cannot build a flourishing life alone. God wisely designed us to need others— in fact, one of His favorite ways to strengthen us is through each other. Look for other couples around you who are also pursuing a thriving marriage. Learn from them, and lean on them.

Get Back Up

There is no such thing as a perfect person or couple! No one gets it right 100 percent of the time. Be prepared when setbacks come. When you have a rough day, just get back up. Ask for forgiveness. It's amazing how a simple, genuine apology can wipe the slate clean. Remember, we're always one step away from heading back in the right direction. Growth is a journey. Ask any thriving couple who's been married longer than you; we guarantee they will tell you they, too, got there one step at a time. Often it looks like taking one step forward, and two steps back. Be encouraged. You're in good company. Trust the God who's leading you. Trust in the power of consistency. Trust that you're headed somewhere *good*!

> Trust in the power of consistency.

Speak Life Over Yourself

Take an inventory of the daily thoughts that are motivating your actions. Are they positive or negative? What beliefs may be derailing your progress? Do you believe a thriving marriage is possible for you? Do you believe God is strong enough to heal your marriage? Do you believe His ways will lead you to the life you long for? Be aware of any thoughts that may be sabotaging your efforts to move toward a thriving marriage, and replace them with the truth of God's Word.

Review

Keep coming back to the "rhythm of us" you crafted for review and reassessment. As we learned in chapter 2, we resist the drift by keeping the truth we have learned continually in front of us. Keep your rhythms where you can see them throughout your day.

It's also important to reassess your rhythm as seasons change. Just as your life together as a couple is always changing and growing, so will the ways in which you can intentionally live out your highest values. Let your rhythm serve you, not the other way around. Keep returning to it for tweaks and changes as needed.

A BLESSING
FOR THE JOURNEY

Stand at the crossroads and look;
ask for the ancient paths,
ask where the good way is, and walk in it,
and you will find rest for your souls.

JEREMIAH 6:16

SO, FRIEND, AS YOU CLOSE THIS BOOK and begin to practice these rhythms of a thriving marriage . . . as the Lord leads you on together, along the *good, ancient* way, may your love for each other bring you unfathomable peace and joy. May it cause those around you to stop and take great notice. May your eyes light up when she walks into the room, may you continue to laugh at his cheesy jokes, and may you always genuinely enjoy one another. May you be found still wildly in love after decades of marriage.

May the thriving rhythms you choose to fill your life with live on well beyond your years. May you cultivate the kind of marriage, family, and life that your wildest dreams are made of. May the legacy of your life together be an invaluable gift to those around you. When your kids grow up and leave home, to enter the world and find spouses of their own, may their genuine desire be *Lord, let me love like that!*

May you live a life of more than just skimming by. May you resist the drift of the current around you and intentionally steward well the precious gift of each other, of this life you've been given together, and may you always see it for the incredible miracle it truly is. May the Lord transform your marriage as you intentionally fill your life with the things you both value most. When the hard days come, as they always do, with God as your unwavering guide, may you always remind each other of the life you long to live and the practices that will get you there.

There are a thousand different ways you can choose to live your life together. May you intentionally center your lives around the rhythms that lead you toward God and toward each other.

Here's to the miracle of marriage.
Here's to grace and strength for your beautiful journey.
Here's to *the rhythm of us.*

JOURNALING PAGES

ACKNOWLEDGMENTS

LOVE AND THANKS TO our wonderful families, the Heflins and the Graebes. We are so blessed to call you ours!

Special thanks to our dear friend Don Pape for listening to the Lord's prompting and reaching out to spark the dream for this project in our hearts. God knew we needed someone with your expertise to even suggest we were capable of such a brave, new adventure. Thank you for believing in, praying for, and encouraging us along the way. We are forever grateful.

This project came to be not in regular daily rhythms of writing (as we would have chosen), but rather in fits and starts. In early mornings and late nights. In stolen hours here and there. And in a few long, glorious weekends, spent mostly surrounded by the beautiful trees at The Brooks at Weatherford (Texas) and Bear Creek, Tennessee. We are so grateful to my (Jenni's) parents, Steve and Tricia, for so generously offering these breathtaking settings for us to enjoy a quiet place to put pen to paper. You have always been the ultimate example of love and generosity to us. Thank you doesn't come close to cutting it for the gift that you both are in our lives. We love you so much!

Thanks and love to my mom, Tricia, for the million hours spent watching your granddaughters so this book could become a reality. They are all better for time spent with Grammie! We're so thankful for you!

A thousand thanks to our lovely, wise, and patient editor, Caitlyn, for believing so much in this message and for asking the right questions to make this project better. You are the actual best! To our copy editor Elizabeth: Your meticulous attention to detail blew us away! To the entire team at NavPress and Tyndale House: We are forever grateful for the honor of partnering with you to make much of Jesus and His incredible rhythms for marriage.

Thanks and much love to our lifer friends whose friendship has carried us through this journey and beyond! Especially to Noah and Erin Labhart, Jordan and Jenna Vandiver, Ian and Lauren Brennfoerder, just to name a few. Your friendship, prayers, and support mean the world to us, and we are forever grateful for you all. #texasforever

Thank you to our dear friend and gifted photographer Meshali Mitchell, for using your amazing gift to capture such a beautiful cover shot. You are the best!

Thank you to our wonderful author friends who wisely guided and faithfully cheered us on as we navigated the continual ups and downs and twists and turns of the writing life. We have learned so much from you—thank you for teaching us well! Special thanks to John and Stasi Eldredge, Kay Wyma, Christy Nockles, Jeannie Cunnion, Kristin Hill, and Gabe and Rebekah Lyons. Your advice, prayers, and support have been the greatest gift.

Thank you to Michael and Linda Adler, our original marriage mentors, for living out the gospel through your marriage. For staying wildly in love for decades. For inspiring everyone who knows you that a lifetime of love is actually possible. We love you both!

Lastly, all our love to our phenomenal kids: Kaden, Addie, Averi, Kennedi, and Keris. You are the absolute light of our lives. Being your mom and dad is our very favorite thing we get to do. Thank you for filling our life with so much awe and wonder. You are our greatest adventure!

NOTES

INTRODUCTION: WE WON'T GET THERE BY ACCIDENT

1. *Merriam-Webster*, "Words We're Watching: 'Xennial,'" accessed May 12, 2021, https://www.merriam-webster.com/words-at-play/words-were-watching-xennial.
2. Eugene H. Peterson, *Christ Plays in Ten Thousand Places: A Conversation in Spiritual Theology* (Grand Rapids, MI: Eerdmans, 2005), 334.
3. Mary Oliver, "The Summer Day," *House of Light* (Boston: Beacon Press, 1990).
4. As cited by Anthem Church, https://www.anthemventura.org/rule.
5. John Eldredge, "45. John Eldredge: Make Space for Your Soul," interview by Chris and Jenni Graebe, *Live It Well* (podcast), September 4, 2019, https://onelife.works/john-eldredge-make-space-for-your-soul/.
6. Ronald Rolheiser, *Domestic Monastery* (Brewster, MA: Paraclete Press, 2019), 41.
7. Rolheiser, *Domestic Monastery*, 44.
8. Margaret Guenther, *At Home in the World: A Rule of Life for the Rest of Us* (New York: Seabury Books, 2006), 30.
9. Guenther, *At Home*, 30.

1: THE FUTURE US

1. Larry Crabb, *Real Church: Does It Exist? Can I Find It?* (Nashville: Thomas Nelson, 2009), 137.
2. Johnnyswim, "Let It Matter," *Georgica Pond* © 2016 Big Picnic Records.

3. Dr. Kevin Leman in "Discovering the Secrets to a Lifelong Romance," *Focus on the Family* broadcast, December 21, 2020, https://www.focusonthefamily.com/episodes/broadcast/discovering-the-secrets-to-a-lifelong-romance-part-1-of-2/.

2: IN MY HEAD

1. *Merriam-Webster*, s.v. "drift, *v.*," accessed May 11, 2021, https://www.merriam-webster.com/dictionary/drift.

2. Blue Letter Bible, "Lexicon: Strong's H6213—*'āśâ*," accessed April 12, 2021, https://www.blueletterbible.org/lang/lexicon/lexicon.cfm?Strongs=H6213&t=NIV.

3. Blue Letter Bible, "Lexicon: Strong's H2896— *tôb*," accessed April 12, 2021, https://www.blueletterbible.org/lang/lexicon/lexicon.cfm?Strongs=H2896&t=NIV.

4. Daniel Harkavy, "Stop Drifting and Get the Life You Want: How Life Planning Can Lead to Real Change," *Forbes*, December 13, 2019, https://www.forbes.com/sites/forbescoachescouncil/2019/12/13/stop-drifting-and-get-the-life-you-want-how-life-planning-can-lead-to-real-change/?sh=460834fa19d2.

5. Eugene H. Peterson, *Under the Unpredictable Plant: An Exploration in Vocational Holiness* (Grand Rapids, MI: Eerdmans, 1992), 35.

6. Eugene H. Peterson, *The Contemplative Pastor: Returning to the Art of Spiritual Direction* (Grand Rapids, MI: Eerdmans, 1993), 23.

7. This process is called "weathering," which our friends Eric and Kristin Hill write about in their book *The First Breakfast: A Journey with Jesus and Peter through Calling, Brokenness, and Restoration* (Milton, GA: Withyou Ministries, 2019).

8. John C. Maxwell, *Success One Day at a Time* (Nashville: J. Countryman, 2000), 7.

3: LETTING GO

1. Blue Letter Bible, "Lexicon: Strong's H4383—*mikšôl*," accessed April 13, 2021, https://www.blueletterbible.org/lang/lexicon/lexicon.cfm?Strongs=H4383&t=NLT.

2. Henry Cloud, *The One-Life Solution: Reclaim Your Personal Life While Achieving Greater Professional Success* (New York: Harper Business, 2011), 151.

3. Cloud, *One-Life Solution*, 153.

4. Marshall Goldsmith, *What Got You Here Won't Get You There: How Successful People Become Even More Successful!* (New York: Hyperion, 2007).

5. Janice Peterson, "54. Janice Peterson: A Life Well Lived," interview

by Chris and Jenni Graebe, *Live It Well* (podcast), April 23, 2019, https://onelife.works/54-janice-peterson-life-well-lived/.

6. James Taylor, "Shower the People," *In the Pocket* © 1976 Warner Bros.

4: WORDS MATTER

1. John Mark Comer, "A Community of Honor in a Culture of Contempt: Romans 12:13," Bridgetown Church, July 28, 2019, https://bridgetown .church/teaching/community/a-community-of-honor-in-a-culture -of-contempt/.

2. Comer, "A Community of Honor."

3. John Gottman, *The Seven Principles for Making Marriage Work: A Practical Guide from the Country's Foremost Relationships Expert* (New York: Harmony, 2015), 157.

4. Esther Perel, "The Secret to Desire in a Long-Term Relationship," filmed February 2013 in New York, TEDSalon video, 18:48, https:// www.ted.com/talks/esther_perel_the_secret_to_desire_in_a_long _term_relationship.

5. I first heard the insight from this verse in an old Beth Moore sermon, where she did a beautiful job explaining this. I was unable to track down the sermon.

6. Dr. Henry Cloud, *Boundaries for Leaders: Results, Relationships, and Being Ridiculously in Charge* (New York: HarperCollins, 2013), 61.

7. Martin Luther King Jr., *A Gift of Love: Sermons from Strength to Love and Other Preachings* (Boston: Beacon Press, 2012), 49.

5: TEAM US

1. Michael and Linda Adler, "3. Loving and Living Well with Michael and Linda Adler," interview by Chris and Jenni Graebe, *Live It Well* (podcast), December 11, 2017, https://onelife.works/olp-ep-3-micheal -and-linda-adler/.

2. Janice Peterson, *Becoming Gertrude: How Our Friendships Shape Our Faith* (Colorado Springs: NavPress, 2018), 1–2.

3. Pastor Michael Adler.

4. As quoted in *Rainbow in the Cloud: The Wisdom and Spirit of Maya Angelou* (New York: Random House, 2014), 78.

5. Eva Van Prooyen, "This One Thing Is the Biggest Predictor of Divorce," Gottman Institute, August 25, 2017, https://www.gottman.com/blog /this-one-thing-is-the-biggest-predictor-of-divorce/.

6. Tim Keller with Kathy Keller, *The Meaning of Marriage: Facing the Complexities of Commitment with the Wisdom of God* (New York: Penguin Books, 2016), 178.

7. Eugene H. Peterson, *The Pastor: A Memoir* (New York: HarperOne, 2012), 37.

8. Henry Cloud, Boundaries.Me course.
9. Dave Ramsey Show (@RamseyShow), "It doesn't matter if you're a Nerd or a Free Spirit. Love makes up the difference. #ValentinesDay," Twitter, February 14, 2013, https://twitter.com/RamseyShow/status /302169813285994500.

6: STEP INTO THE PAINTING

1. Mark and Jan Foreman, "17. Raising Brave Kids with Mark and Jan Foreman," interview by Chris and Jenni Graebe, *Live It Well* (podcast), March 12, 2018, https://onelife.works/17-raising-brave-kids-mark -jan-foreman/.
2. Mark and Jan Foreman, "17. Raising Brave Kids."
3. Ronald Rolheiser, *Forgotten among the Lilies: Learning to Love Beyond Our Fears* (New York: Doubleday, 2005), 115.
4. Rolheiser, *Forgotten among the Lilies*, 115.
5. Ellie Lisitsa, "An Introduction to Emotional Bids and Trust," *Gottman Relationship Blog*, August 31, 2012, https://www.gottman.com/blog /an-introduction-to-emotional-bids-and-trust/#:~:text=John %20Gottman%20calls%20your%20Emotional,commitment %20to%20supporting%20each%20other.
6. John Gottman and Nan Silver, *What Makes Love Last? How to Build Trust and Avoid Betrayal* (New York: Simon & Schuster Paperbacks, 2013), 101.
7. Eugene H. Peterson, *The Contemplative Pastor: Returning to the Art of Spiritual Direction* (Grand Rapids, MI: Eerdmans, 1993), 115.
8. As quoted in John Mark Comer, *The Ruthless Elimination of Hurry* (Colorado Springs: WaterBrook, 2019), 19.

7: STAY AWAKE AND ALIVE

1. Henry Cloud, *9 Things You Simply Must Do to Succeed in Love and Life: A Psychologist Probes the Mystery of Why Some Lives Really Work and Others Don't* (Nashville: Thomas Nelson, 2004), 41.
2. Noah and Erin Labhart, "13. Being Brave Together with Noah and Erin Labhart," interview by Chris and Jenni Graebe, *Live It Well* (podcast), February 12, 2018, https://onelife.works/13-brave-together/.
3. Mark and Jan Foreman, "17. Raising Brave Kids with Mark and Jan Foreman," interview by Chris and Jenni Graebe, *Live It Well* (podcast), March 12, 2018, https://onelife.works/17-raising-brave-kids-mark -jan-foreman/.
4. Richard Leider and Steven Buchholz, "The Rustout Syndrome," *Training & Development* 49, no. 3 (March 1995): 7.
5. Leider and Buchholz, "The Rustout Syndrome": 7.
6. As quoted in *Pocket Maya Angelou Wisdom: Inspirational Quotes and*

Wise Words from a Legendary Icon (London: Hardie Grant Books, 2019), 85.

7. John Eldredge, *The Journey of Desire: Searching for the Life You've Always Dreamed Of*, expanded ed. (Nashville: Nelson Books, 2016), 51.

8. John Eldredge, *The Journey of Desire*, 66.

9. A. W. Tozer, *The Pursuit of God*, updated edition (Abbotsford, WI: Aneko Press, 2015), 3.

10. Tyler Staton, Church Outside the Gate, Oaks Church Brooklyn.

11. Jon Levy, "The Science Behind How Adventure Can Save Your Life," *Fortune*, May 3, 2017, https://fortune.com/2017/05/03/adventure-jon-levy-health/.

12. Jon Levy, "385. The Art and Science of Epic Adventure with Jon Levy," interview with Lewis Howes, *The School of Greatness* (podcast), September 26, 2016, https://lewishowes.com/podcast/jon-levy/.

13. John O'Donohue, *To Bless the Space Between Us: A Book of Blessings* (New York: Doubleday, 2008), 26.

14. Steve and Sarah Dubbeldam, "57. Steve and Sarah Dubbeldam: Believe in Each Other's Dreams," interview by Chris and Jenni Graebe, *Live It Well* (podcast), June 3, 2019, https://onelife.works/57-steve-and-sarah-dubbeldam-believe-in-each-others-dreams/.

15. Wes Yoder, *Bond of Brothers: Connecting with Other Men Beyond Work, Weather, and Sports* (Grand Rapids, MI: Zondervan, 2010), 100.

16. John and Stasi Eldredge, *Captivating: Unveiling the Mystery of a Woman's Soul*, revised and expanded (Nashville: Thomas Nelson, 2010), 12.

17. Personal conversation with Michael Adler.

18. Katherine Wolf, "85. Katherine Wolf: Suffer Strong," interview by Chris and Jenni Graebe, June 30, 2020, https://onelife.works/85-katherine-wolf-suffer-strong/.

8: FRESH EYES

1. Mark and Jan Foreman, "17. Raising Brave Kids with Mark and Jan Foreman," interview by Chris and Jenni Graebe, *Live It Well* (podcast), March 12, 2018, https://onelife.works/17-raising-brave-kids-mark-jan-foreman/.

2. This saying is from a beloved Sunday School teacher of mine, Don Wideman.

3. Jonah Berger, *Contagious: Why Things Catch On* (New York: Simon & Schuster, 2016), 106.

4. As quoted in Berger, *Contagious*, 102.

5. Paul Piff and Dacher Keltner, "Why Do We Experience Awe?" *New York Times* May 22, 2015, https://www.nytimes.com/2015/05/24/opinion/sunday/why-do-we-experience-awe.html#:~:text=Years%20ago%2C%20one%20of%20us,that%20enhance%20the%20greater%20good

.&text=They%20gave%20approximately%2040%20percent,participants
%20who%20were%20awe%2Ddeprived.

6. Timothy Keller with Katherine Leary Alsdorf, *Every Good Endeavor: Connecting Your Work to God's Work* (New York: Penguin Books, 2016), 165.

7. Gary Thomas, "64. Gary Thomas: Know When to Walk Away," interview by Chris and Jenni Graebe, *Live It Well* (podcast), October 15, 2019, https://onelife.works/64-gary-thomas-know-when-to-walk-away/.

8. Hyman Judah Schachtel, *The Real Enjoyment of Living* (New York: Dutton, 1954), 37.

9. John Gottman, *Why Marriages Succeed or Fail: And How You Can Make Yours Last* (New York: Simon & Schuster, 1994), 79–80.

10. John M. Gottman and Nan Silver, *The Seven Principles for Making Marriage Work: A Practical Guide from the Country's Foremost Relationship Expert* (New York: Harmony Books, 2015), 22–23. As Gottman acknowledges, the concepts of "positive sentiment override" and "negative sentiment override" were coined by psychologist Robert Weiss.

11. Henry Cloud, "Envy vs. Real Desire," Facebook video, May 16, 2018, https://www.facebook.com/watch/?v=10156490237404571.

12. Eugene H. Peterson, *A Long Obedience in the Same Direction: Discipleship in an Instant Society* (Downers Grove, IL: IVP, 2021), 94.

13. Tom Hanks as Jimmy Dugan in *A League of Their Own* (Culver City, CA: Columbia Pictures, 1992), VHS.

14. Francis Frangipane, *The Shelter of the Most High: Living Your Life Under the Divine Protection of God* (Lake Mary, FL: Charisma House, 2008), 117.

15. Frangipane, *Shelter of the Most High*, 117–118.

16. Abraham Joshua Heschel, "Celebration," in *The Wisdom of Heschel*, selected by Ruth Marcus Goodhill (New York: Farrar, Straus and Giroux, 1975), 152.

17. This is a form of the Examen Prayer—a way we have found to practice it together as a couple at the end of the day.

18. As explained in Andy Tix, "The Next Eastern Therapy: 'Forest Bathing' Has the Potential to Be the Next Big Health Craze," *Psychology Today*, May 23, 2016, https://www.psychologytoday.com/us/blog/the-pursuit-peace/201605/the-next-eastern-therapy. Referenced study: Paul K. Piff et al., "Awe, the Small Self, and Prosocial Behavior," *Journal of Personality and Social Psychology* 108, no. 6 (June 2015): 883–99.

19. Bryan E. Robinson, "What Are 'Awe Walks?': And Why Is a New Study Praising Them?" *Psychology Today*, November 3, 2020, https://www.psychologytoday.com/us/blog/the-right-mindset/202011/what-are-awe-walks.

20. Sarah Dillon, "Doing This for 15 Minutes Every Day Can Improve Your Overall Happiness," *News Break* September 23, 2020, https:// www.newsbreak.com/news/2067911181006/doing-this-for-15-minutes -every-day-can-improve-your-overall-happiness.
21. Tyler Staton, Ash Wednesday service, Oaks Church Brooklyn, February 17, 2021.
22. G. K. Chesterton, "The Advantages of Having One Leg," in *On Lying in Bed and Other Essays*, ed. Alberto Manguel (Calgary, Alberta, Canada: Bayeux Arts, 2000), 32.

9: UNCOVER YOUR VALUES

1. Mark Murphy, "Neuroscience Explains Why You Need to Write Down Your Goals If You Actually Want to Achieve Them," *Forbes*, April 15, 2018, https://www.forbes.com/sites/markmurphy/2018/04/15 /neuroscience-explains-why-you-need-to-write-down-your-goals -if-you-actually-want-to-achieve-them/?sh=6b135a3c7905.

EPILOGUE: A BRAND-NEW DAY

1. Pastor Tom Nelson, Denton Bible Church.
2. Erwin Raphael McManus, *The Last Arrow: Save Nothing for the Next Life* (New York: Waterbrook, 2017), 9.